The Dome of Silence

Sexual Harassment and Abuse in Sport

Sandra Kirby,
Lorraine Greaves
and Olena Hankivsky

Fernwood Publishing
Zed Books

Editing: Brenda Conroy
Cover photo: Wayne Clowacki, Winnipeg Free Press Collection, Western Canada Pictorial Index
Design and production: Beverley Rach
Printed and bound in Canada by: Hignell Printing Limited

Published in Canada by Fernwood Publishing Ltd.
Box 9409, Station A
Halifax, Nova Scotia
B3K 5S3

Published in the rest of the world by Zed Books Ltd.
7 Cynthia Street, London NI 9JF
Distributed in the USA exclusively by Palgrave,
a division of St. Martins Press, LLC, 175 Fifth Ave., New York, 10010, USA.

Zed Books
ISBN 1 85649 963 4 Paper
ISBN 1 85649 962 6 Cloth

Fernwood Publishing Company Limited gratefully acknowledges the financial support of the Department of Canadian Heritage and the Canada Council for the Arts for our publishing program.

Every effort was made to secure permission to reprint copyright material. On page 24, the text from "Crossing the Line," CBC, *The Fifth Estate*, Nov. 2, 1993, is used with the permission of David Studer, Executive Producer. The Paul Hickson story on page 34, is reprinted with permission of The Associated Press.
The Maple Leaf Gardens Scandal on page 101 uses quotes from the original "Lives Lived" column with the permission of the author, James Macgowan.

British CIP available from the British Library

Canadian Cataloguing in Publication Data

Main entry under title:

The dome of silence

ISBN 1-55266-035-4

1. Sexual harassment of women. 2. Women athletes -- Abuse of. 3. Sports -- Moral and ethical aspects. I. Kirby, Sandra L. (Sandra Louise), 1949- II. Greaves, Lorraine. III. Hankivsky, Olena.

HQ1237.D65 2000   305.43'796   C00-950120-7

Contents

Dedication

We would like to dedicate this to those athletes who have had the courage to speak out about sexual harassment and abuse in sport and to all the volunteers who work in the best interests of athletes.

We also dedicate this to the late Sgt. Gordon Allen Kirby; JoAnn Leavey; and Roma and Basyl Hankivsky.

Acknowledgements

First and foremost, we would like to thank Canada's high performance and Olympic athletes for responding to a very atypical survey, one about sexual harassment and abuse in sport. Without their thoughtful responses, this book would not have been possible and our understanding of sexual harassment and abuse amongst these and other athletes would be much poorer. We would also like to thank Sport Canada for having the foresight and the courage to fund such research well before such research was "a good thing to be doing."

This book takes its place in the rapidly expanding field of sexual harassment and abuse studies in sport, most notably those by Celia Brackenridge (e.g. *Spoilsports: Understanding and preventing Sexual Exploitation in Sport*, forthcoming), Kari Fasting, Brackenridge and Borgen (*Sexual Harassment In and Outside Sport*, 2000), Mariah Burton Nelson (*The Unburdened Heart*, 2000) and Laura Robinson (*Crossing the Line*, 1998). It is our communication with these and other authors that has made this book both possible and timely. In addition to the above authors, we would like to thank WomenSport International's Task Force on Sexual Harassment in Sport, Hugette Dagenais of Recherches Feministes, and Karin More of the British Columbia Centre of Excellence for Women's Health.

While working on this book we have been institutionally supported by the University of Winnipeg and the British Columbia Centre of Excellence for Women's Health. Our colleagues in these programs have variously supported us, queried our progress, kept us on track and now, will be so glad that we are done.

We gratefully acknowledge the contributions to the development of this book by our editor at Fernwood Publishing. Anonymous readers also provided some valuable feedback on the draft version of this manuscript.

Preface

by Celia Brackenridge
(Professor of Sport and Leisure,
Cheltenham and Gloucester College of Higher Education, U.K.)

When the Ben Johnson doping scandal hit the world's headlines at the 1988 Olympic Games Canadians determined that they would never again face international humiliation in sport. The Dubin Inquiry was established to clean up Canadian sport, to restate the ethical values which are supposed to underpin modern sport and to guarantee that the highest possible moral standards would be upheld in sport thereafter. But it was to be only a few years before a new scandal was to emerge which would wreak even greater devastation on the wider sport community—sexual abuse of athletes.

Sexual abuse and harassment in sport are not new phenomena: both male and female athletes have suffered sexual degradation from their peers, coaches and others for decades, through hazing and initiation rituals, domineering training regimes and thought control processes. Yet, as this book argues, the dome of silence has operated effectively to reinforce both personal and organizational denial. It is no accident that it has taken so long to turn the attention of national and international sport organizations to this problem for, despite some ten or more years of academic research into sexual abuse and harassment in sport, the dominant discourses in sport in the 1990s have been about money, markets and medals.

The revelations about the abuse of Sheldon Kennedy in Canadian professional ice hockey, and rapes perpetrated by former Great Britain Olympic swimming coach Paul Hickson, have shocked their respective countries. Often it takes a major incident involving a famous name, such as these, to trigger an institutional response. Shock leads first to denial then to anger and, finally, to action. So, while such incidents often destroy the self-esteem, family relationships and sport potential of individuals, in the longer term they do raise the profile of the issue and bring about the prospects of positive change. That is small consolation for those athletes whose sporting careers have been wrecked, who have never found the strength to speak out or who have been ridiculed or ostracized for doing so.

Former elite athlete and contemporary writer Mariah Burton Nelson first broke the public taboo about sexual abuse in sport in her prize

8

award book, *Are We Winning Yet? How Sports are Changing Women and Women are Changing Sports* (Random House, 1991) in a chapter entitled, "My coach says he loves me." She went on to develop her arguments about violence and gender relations in sport in her sequel, *The Stronger Women Get, the More Men Love Football* (Aven Books, 1995). The first academic studies of sexual harassment and abuse in sport, in the mid to late 1980s and early 1990s, were based mainly on small samples and/or qualitative research designs. This book breaks new ground. Here, for the first time, the authors present systematic, statistical data from a national survey of sexual harassment and abuse amongst current and former Canadian Olympians and link their findings to wider debates on the prevalence of sexual violence in modern life.

Sandra Kirby, Lorraine Greaves and Olena Hankivsky are ideally suited to write this book. Between them, they represent all the audiences who have a stake in making sexual abuse vanish from our sporting landscape—the parent, the coach, the politician, the fan, the sport organizer and, of course, the athlete. All are committed feminists with a background in advocacy and political activism for the betterment of women and society; all are engaged in working relentlessly to stem the tide of violence in society, in public and in private spaces; and all have honed the intellectual, research and writing skills which are necessary to convey their work to the world. As a professor of sociology, Sandra Kirby has a wide theoretical and methodological repertoire from which to draw her analysis; as a health advocate, Lorraine Greaves is perfectly placed to set the study of sexual harassment and abuse in sport within a wider social context and as a political scientist, Olena Hankivsky brings her acute analytical skills to both sport and social policy.

All three authors recognize a great deal more research is needed before we can judge the true extent of sexual abuse in different sport, at all levels of participation. Yet practical interventions in sport do not have to wait for years of research. Some sport organizations in Canada and in Great Britain have begun the painful process of looking in the organizational mirror, analyzing and reviewing their behaviour then changing their methods and practices. This book should help to accelerate that process of change.

Recognizing that sexual abuse occurs in sport requires no more than recognizing that sport is simply part of society. But the old myth about sport as a moral oasis still has currency. If the public and those who run our major sport organizations are reluctant to confront racism, sexism and homophobia in sport, as they still are, then it is no surprise that they struggle to confront sexual abuse. All of these are widespread, systematic problems in sport today, the result of generations of selective attention to the rewards of sport and selective blindness to the human processes it engages.

This book is a shocking indictment of modern sport. For some, it will touch a raw nerve and reawaken painful personal experiences but it may also provide them with the confidence to disclose these experiences for the first time. Others will be disgusted or angered by what they read. It is also to be hoped that some readers will pause to reflect on their own behaviours, their own expectations of sport and their own uncritical submission to the culture of winning.

Celia Brackenridge
Cheltenham and Gloucester College of Higher Education, U.K.

Chapter One

The Problem of Sexual Abuse in Sport

Sheldon Kennedy was just fourteen years old when he first met Graham James, his Canadian Junior Hockey League coach. By 1996, at age forty-four, James had been named the Coach of the Year and his team, the Swift Current Broncos, had won the prestigious Memorial Cup. In September of the same year, James suddenly resigned his coaching position amidst charges of sexual abuse of two of his players. One of the players was Sheldon Kennedy. As it turned out, James had groomed Kennedy for abuse by controlling his hockey career, schooling and leisure activities. Kennedy had been sexually assaulted more than three hundred times, apparently without anyone being suspicious. Kennedy had been silent about the abuse because of the macho environment in ice hockey, and, because James was such a winning coach, he felt no one would listen.

Sexual abuse in sport has been a condition with no name or face. The recent and brave efforts of Canadian athletes such as Sheldon Kennedy have betrayed the silence that has, for decades, been clamped over sport. This book is about that silence—what it has hidden, why it has persisted so long, and how it may be encouraged to lift. This will not be easy. The "dome" of silence over sexual abuse in sport laces together several imperatives of Western democratic culture into a unique and tight cover. Retracting that dome will take concerted effort and collaborative will.

Sexual abuse in the sport context is much like sexual abuse in other social institutions; it is debilitating, shaming, isolating and traumatic to its victims. Our understanding of the full impact of sexual abuse in sport is helped by over two decades of extensive research on violence, particularly its etiology and its effects on women and children. Adding to this, we reflect on the unique aspects of the sport context that have contributed to sexual abuse and harassment and to the resounding silence surrounding it. We hope this will lead us to a greater understanding of why sport has been one of the last social institutions to avoid scrutiny and of how the silence may be broken.

Crucial to uncovering this problem are the voices of the Canadian athletes reported in this book. In 1996, with the financial support of Sport Canada and the assistance of the Canadian Athletes Association, we surveyed all of the members, both male and female, of the Canadian

The Case of Graham James (Hockey Coach and later General Manager of a Junior Ice-Hockey Team) As compiled by Carolyn Fusco and Sandra Kirby, 2000.
1952-1996:
1952: Graham James born in Prince Edward Island.
1970: James quits playing hockey, begins coaching. One assault charge dates from this period.
1984: Graham James meets Sheldon Kennedy, a fourteen-year-old player with professional hockey potential. In 1984, a group of players "demanded that James be fired because his sexuality was having a negative effect on his coaching" (Mitchell, *Globe and Mail*, Jan. 14, 1997:A1).
1986-1994: James is coach and general manager for the Swift Current Broncos. In a 1986 bus accident, four players die. During this time, Kennedy says about James that "it was like I was his wife or his lover" (Mapine, *Calgary Herald*).
1992: James charged with assault when, during a hockey game, he physically retaliated against a fan.
1996: On April 17, Kennedy told other players about the sexual abuse he had suffered at the hands of James (Board, *Edmonton Journal*). Kennedy gave the police a "statement of fact" (Aug. 23). Shortly afterwards, James resigns as coach of the Calgary Hitmen (Sept. 5), police confirm they are investigating James (Sept. 6) and the first public notice of charges is given (Sept. 7). Alan Adams' *Toronto Star* article appears on Oct. 23. Kennedy breaks a long-standing tradition of secrecy and releases his name to the Calgary press (Oct. 29), and charges are laid against James on Nov. 22. Adams (*Toronto Star*) provides the first major national coverage of the story, raising issues of pedophiles on the Internet, criminal screening of coaches, and the "allegations" of James' misconduct."

1997:
January 2: James pleads guilty to two counts of sexual assault and one count of indecent assault, from 1984-1994, against Kennedy and two unnamed players. He is to be jailed for three and a half years.
January 3: Five stories in major newspapers, four on the front page, three accompanied by photographs of James. Two players are victims but no names are included in the press coverage. The first mention is made of the actual pattern of abuse Kennedy suffered (each Tuesday and Thursday night), the frequency of abuse (Kennedy suffered more than 300 assaults, the other player about 50) and the type of abuse (mutual masturbation, attempt at oral and anal sex, the use of a gun). Kennedy, who was fourteen years old when the assaults began, once eluded James by running home in his hockey equipment, the other player finally had a fist fight with James to make him stop. James is reported in the *Calgary Herald* as saying he was a homosexual and that other players had accepted his advances. James' lawyer was reported as saying that James "made an incredible error in judgement" (Mapina, *Calgary Herald*). The hockey community's reaction is one of surprise and shock, although there had been numerous rumours about James. The issue of hockey management foreknowledge and inaction is first raised.
January 4: Two stories, one front page. Both concentrate on child protection initiatives. Comparisons are made between abusers in the church, the military and those in sport.
January 6: Two stories, one front page. An in-depth interview with Kennedy is reported and Kennedy is called "courageous." Kennedy's wife Jana is credited with finally confronting James and encouraging Kennedy to speak out about abuse he experienced.
January 7: Sixteen stories, two front page: the most stories printed in one day and the first international story (*USA Today*). The Kennedy interview is repeated in many of the stories. First appearance of the sexual abuse allegations against Brian Shaw, who is reported to have died of AIDs-related cancer in 1993 (Taylor, *Winnipeg Free Press*). Kennedy is portrayed as a happily married father of one. One of

James' friends reports that "I have known Graham for twenty years ... I'd heard all the rumours that he was gay. But I had no idea he was abusing players" (Taylor, *Winnipeg Free Press*). He also is quoted as saying "What concerns me is that, in the media, there has been an equation of homosexuality with sexual abuse. Just because a person is homosexual doesn't mean he's a sexual predator" (Taylor, *Winnipeg Free Press*).

Also, the first reports of the abuse of a position of power are addressed. James portrayed variously as "sick," a "creep," an "S.O.B.," a pedophile, and the doer of a heinous deed who "had sexual control," "screwed up Kennedy's life" and "stole Kennedy's trust." He is also portrayed as "just a gay man in love with two teenagers" (Allen, *USA Today*).

Kennedy portrayed as a child whose youth was stolen. Kennedy was afraid to say anything because "It was like we were married" (Presse Canadienne, *Le journal de Quebec*); and that the public would just "portray you as a gay guy and nothing will come of it [the accusation]" (McCarten, *Globe and Mail*). Reports first emerge about Kennedy's difficulties with alcohol. He is quoted as saying "Il (James) a bousille' toute ma vie."

Kirby and Greaves article "The Dome of Silence" referred to under-reporting of male sexual abuse experiences. Also, there seems to be some evidence of the lack of concern by the hockey organization once the sexual abuse was reported.

January 8: Fifteen stories, no front page though three are front page of the sports section. Items include Don Cherry's comments about James being at the "bottom of the totem pole"; the demons within hockey; Kennedy's courage; reluctance of the public to deal with the issue; the existence of sexual predators in sport; government action on codes of conduct, reporting rules and a control registry; the apparently high tolerance for abuse if the coach is "a winning coach"; the ongoing lack of attention to sexual abuse of adolescent girls in sport.

James is quoted as saying "I guess I just wished it were acceptable. Maybe I thought I was living in Ancient Greece or something like that ... I only crossed the line a couple of times" (Spector, *Edmonton Journal*).

One newspaper is searching for the identity of the other high profile player among the victims and reports that there could be as many as twenty-five other victims.

The *Washington Post* reports on the courage of Kennedy and that despite his comment, "You don't have a clue what to do ... I always felt like I was *not normal*," no victim needs to feel ashamed. They also present hockey as "a natural puberty right ... in the contest of elemental machismo" for young males. With millions of players trying to get into the National Hockey League, players 17–19 years old in the junior leagues play more than seventy games in a season. The James' case is seen as "A Tear in Canada's Fabric."

January 9: Five stories, one front page. The language in these stories begins to get ugly: e.g. "creeps" (Christie, *Globe and Mail*) "every ugly piece of information raises even darker possibilities"; the sex abuse scandal was a "stomach wrenching knife in the solar plexis"; "this sickly tale of shattered faith and predatory abuse" and "James was confronted by players for his homosexuality and blatant and disturbing behaviour" (Make, *Vancouver Sun*). One story concentrated on what the public could do to be vigilant and to protect their children because the "danger (of people like James) always lurks" (Engler, *Vancouver Sun*). One story was an exposé on Brian Shaw, his pattern of showering with "his boys," his death due to AIDs-related cancer in 1993 and his role in the governance of hockey. The point was that Shaw was gay and abused players for years with impunity, an open secret. The author writes that this signalled to James that he also could abuse players with impunity (Houston and Campbell, *Globe and Mail*).

Perhaps the most interesting from our perspective is that "(w)hat has held back the exposure of much of the abuse has been the element of denial: denial that something as wholesome as sport can harbour predators and creeps, denial that youngsters have the same rights and integrity in a sports arena as they have on the street" (Shoalts, *Globe and Mail*). There was also the assertion that some athletes "try on their sexuality with coaches, flirting and touching" (Christie, *Globe and Mail*).

January 10: Five articles, none front page. The focus is on Kennedy, the only identifiable victim. His story is presented as that of an innocent farm boy who was "forced to share the coach's bed and engage in perverse and degrading acts" (*The Gazette*). His decade of anguish was described. It is reiterated that Kennedy thought he was gay because he was abused by James. The story of Shaw is again presented, this time from the view of the hockey management. With no one coming forward and without proof the management could not act. The focus seems to be on the recovery of the sport by concentrating on family values (Editorial, *The Gazette*).

Kennedy says his time with James was "like we were married or something" and that James kept Kennedy with him on all trips. Kennedy called James a very smart and manipulative man. Hockey "is sacred hallowed ground," a religion to some, "a balm for the soul of the nation" (Vecsey, dePalma, *New York Times*).

January 11: The number of articles is beginning to drop off. Four articles, one front page. These feature the response of the Canadian Hockey Association. Costello, the President says that "I'm sure that people of this deviant nature can burrow into an organization and pick a spot for strange ways" (Bray, *The Gazette*). Costello recognized that although hockey harboured men like James and Shaw, the deviants (pedophiles) should go elsewhere but not in hockey.

One article, (Make, *The Ottawa Citizen*), suggested that James had already selected his next teenaged victim by establishing an RRSP out of his own money for the player and taking him on out-of-town trips.

January 13: Three articles, one front page. The world of pedophilia collides with the wholesome world of hockey. The first mention of hazing rituals (Wong, *Globe and Mail*) and the conditions in which players travelled (isolated from friends, cramped buses, lots of touching, macho atmosphere) and that it would be impossible in these conditions for a player "to come out of the closet." Press reports a common homophobic locker room joke ("How would you know if a player was gay? He ties his skates on with his legs crossed!")

Don Cherry says that "coaches who prey on children should be drawn and quartered" and that others should be castrated or get life in prison (Denley, *The Ottawa Citizen*). This same author is among the first to draw the distinction between sexual orientation and men aroused by children and points out that most pedophiles are heterosexual men. Pedophilia, homosexuality and bisexuality used in the same paragraph.

Using a University of Ottawa psychologist who works with Corrections Canada in the treatment of sex offenders, *The Ottawa Citizen* describes pedophilia as "a sexual orientation in much the same way that heterosexuality or homosexuality is for others. These men are aroused by children and it's an innate condition, not learned behaviour or moral depravity. ... Men don't choose to be pedophiles." Some "pedophiles are homosexual. Their rate of reoffending is much higher. Some studies show as high as 50%."

January 14: Only two articles, one front page. An element of fearmongering is present—no distinction is made between pedophilia and homosexuality. The public didn't know they were at risk while James fooled many of them. 1994, James dropped all his clothes except for his shorts while he was coaching a game (Mitchell, *Globe and Mail*). James was quoted as "being in love with a young player" (McCarten, *Globe and Mail*).

January 15: Conspiracy of silence in sport is addressed. Most victims are female yet the press does not get on the issue until it is a male player who is abused

January 16: Three articles, none front page. The *Christian Science Monitor* reports about how deep sport is in the North American culture and that revelations of the sexual abuse by James will have "a profound effect on Canadian junior hockey's macho culture" (Clayton). Junior hockey has 1300 players under the age of nineteen years, some 500,000 players aspire to junior hockey teams. The draft is for players under eighteen years of age and "the coach is the door" (Kirby).

Reference to the dark side of hockey where James apparently "routinely paid players to have sex with women while he watched ... their girlfriends or others" (Robinson, 1998; McCarten, *The Vancouver Sun*) and had apparently "picked out his next victim." Conspiracy of silence theme picked up in the *Vancouver Sun*.

January 18: Only one article, an "op ed" piece by Michelle Landsberg, a well-known social commentator. The whole country leaves her "gagging and chocking with fury" and in "a paroxysm of rage and disgust at pedophiles" (*Toronto Star*). She writes that scores of players have been molested by coaches because of public blindness—our refusal to listen. She says that we are "in an endless cycle of revelation and shock ... astounded and shocked anew."

January 20: Three articles, one on the front page of the *Alberta Report*, an infamous right-wing magazine. *Macleans* (Deacon and Nemeth) provides a summary of the events since the January 2 conviction of James. Calls by boys and men to sexual abuse lines have increased fivefold. Kennedy has become very influential and hockey has been "cut to the heart" as the "hockey dream darkens." Other cases (Middleborough, B.C.; Shaw, Portland) are raised and the focus is on the "incredible power" predators have over athletes.

The *Alberta Report* article (Sillers) is a particularly vicious article containing subtitles such as "Depravity in the Dressing Room," "Hockey Pays the Price for Gay Tolerance" and "The Ugly Truth about Predatory Homosexual Coaches Finally Comes Out." Sodomy is in sport's macho culture, Sillers writes, and in an increasingly permissive society, homosexuals run free as they find increased acceptance in sport. Quotes from Gwen Landolt, lawyer and president of REAL Women (right-wing; anti-

equality), Hannon (advocate for intergenerational sex), Don Cherry (producer of a series of videos featuring hockey violence—"Rock 'em Sock 'em Hockey"). Inflammatory phrases used like "sordid scandal, predatory homosexual, "men groping and sodomizing young males," "the triumph of the gay agenda," "limp-wristed players or coaches," James satisfying "his carnal cravings," James as "a ravenous homosexual predator."

Sillers laments that because of human rights protections, "It would be almost impossible to fire a gay hockey coach in Alberta" and accuses the media of "painstakingly downplaying James' homosexuality."

A particularly badly informed article, "Homosexual predation affects women's sport too" is included in *Alberta Report*. Here such quotes as "Females are more likely to abuse power in a sports relationship ... and that problem is acute in sports which have a high percentage of lesbians" (women's hockey, softball and golf); and "the abuse of power for sexual purposes in women's sport is almost always homosexual ... mainly because there are so few women coaching men. It's a hidden side of sport" lead readers to erroneous conclusions. The old stereotype of "lesbian coaches and senior players attempting to recruit newcomers into the gay lifestyle" is particularly odorous. No data is referenced except that these are the opinions of one sports psychologist. Quotes from the text include:

"He reportedly broke down, confessed he was gay and agreed to resign at the end of the season" (p.32, no reference);

"He... seemed to think he could continue preying on vulnerable young men indefinitely" (p.32);

"My problem was I cared too much and got carried away... If the (complainants) didn't see anything wrong with it, than I guess I didn't feel guilty" (p.32);

"These days it is difficult to follow up on rumours of homosexual misconduct because it is politically incorrect to put gays under any kind of critical scrutiny, observes Gwen Landolt. "It opens an organization up to the charge of being 'homophobic,'" observes the lawyer. ... She argues that "the continuing legal and medical acceptance of homosexuality will make the entrenchment of gays and lesbians in minor sport all the more impregnable. Coaches fired for being gay would cry discrimination and likely win" (p.33);

"James thought that his only crime was that he acted from a position of authority" (p.34);

"One of the outcomes of political correctness is that it is all right to expose a homosexual predatory among males, but it is much more difficult to talk about the other side of the coin without being accused of being anti-female" (Smith, in Sillers, p.33);

"Thirty years ago people wouldn't have cared if it were a consensual act or not. They would have said it was wrong and fired the coach." But, in the past few decades, "The homosexual issue has blurred the boundaries of sexual behaviour and morality" (Ferri, in Sillers, p.31);

"When you are in a position of authority, it's best to keep sex out of it." Hannon conceded that to have the case 'vigorously thrust before the nation's eyes ... is just horrifying to people'" (Hannon, supporter of intergenerational sex, p. 31);

"Canadians should brace themselves for more deviants to pop up behind the benches of young hockey players" (Landolt, p. 32);

"To these homosexual predators, the dressing rooms of pubescent boys are no longer off limits" (p.30);

"I'd have drawn and quartered the S.O.B." (Cherry, p.31);

"Under cover of darkness, attempted oral sex, masturbated on the boy's feet and fondled him" (p. 31); "including attempted anal sex" (p.31);

"Kennedy may have been physically strong enough to fight off his molester, coaches wield tremendous psychological power over their players" (p.31);

"It was like I was his wife or his lover ... I believe that Graham truely fell in love with me ... [but] there was no willingness on my part" (Kennedy, p. 32);

"I became the key person in his (Kennedy's) life" (James, p.32);

"James' infatuation with his new companion got a little out of control and was at times 'blatant and disturbing' ... it became overt!" (p.32)

January 22: Two articles, none front page. There is a rejection of a national inquiry, although there is no denial of the problem of sexual harassment and abuse by the sports community. Reason given for the rejection was protection for athletes given how badly it was thought that athletes had been treated in the Dubin Inquiry (an examination of drug abuse in high performance sport). The Canadian Council on Ethics in Sport (CCES) is quoted as saying that sport is about the physical and moral development of youth, and that the duty of care asserts itself. (Note: this can be taken either way—clean up sport, or homosexuality is a moral issue)

January 23: Two articles, one reiterating the rejection of a call for a national inquiry, the other highlighting the longstanding problem of sexual abuse of female athletes. Several cases are cited (Lawrence, *The Vancouver Sun*).

January 29: Two articles in the *Manitoban*, the student paper of the University of Manitoba. Kennedy's history as a player is reiterated and the author (Herstein) concludes that "It is as if no one was molested before." The case of Shaw is brought up and "no one did a bloody thing," just as management did nothing when James "paid his players to have sex with women while he watched." The story has definitely turned ugly. Infers that pubescent players as "confused as hell" and that James thought Kennedy "would never squeal." Author is sickened by whole affair.

January 30: Two articles, none front page. One focuses on the problems in sport (racism at the 1993 Kamloops Winter Games, harassment at the 1995 Canada Winter Games, the CIAU report on harassment (Holman), the Kirby and Greaves study *(Globe and Mail)*. The other focuses on the "pain and shame of Graham James... reprehensible coaches and the wall of silence that successfully ignored the rumblings about Shaw" (Atkinson, *Regina Leader*).

February:
Eight articles, none front page. Kennedy claims back his life and is cited for being the first of twenty-five people in sport who made a difference (Christie and Langford, *Globe and Mail*). "If it was teen-aged girls involved instead of teen-aged boys, alarm bells would surely have sounded by now" (Brunt, *Globe and Mail*). Other cases are brought forward—those in B.C., Newfoundland, Halifax) and reference is made to the Badgley Report on "sexual Offences Against Children (1984), and "society's darker and dirtier corners"; The *Winnipeg Free Press* story (Galloway, Feb.11) of the emotions about gay coaches and misconduct, links between homosexuality and pedophilia ... but although author uses some of the story from the *Alberta Report*, she takes on the myth of the connection and writes that pedophiles don't care about the sex of the child they assault. The *New York Times* (Lapointe) raises the issue of "the sordid underbelly of Canadian hockey" and says that pedophilia is "one of those periodic problems that comes and goes and leaves everything pretty much as it was" (Feb. 23 p.3).

March:
2 articles, none front page. James identified for the first time as a "serial sexual predator" and that as more players come forward, these will lead to "obvious and crippling results"(Kimberly et al., *Calgary Herald*).

April:
One article, not front page. After the revelations about the Maple Leaf Gardens Sexual Abuse scandal (a pedophile ring connected with hockey), in "Protecting Athletes" (Ormsby, *Toronto Star*) uses language like "terrifying children versus curbing their joy ... frightening extent of the problem ... awful ... appalling ... monstrous bogeyman in sport ... paralyzed with fear and gruesome expectations."

  In addition, the Canadian Association for the Advancement of Women and Sport (CAAWS) released its spring edition of *Action* and addressed head-on the issues of gender of the

victim and the perpetrator, the problem of "ridding sport of pedophiles by purging homosexuals from sport" and provides an excellent rationale for homophobia as an issue in sport. Sickened, disgusted, bad days, purge homosexuals, sacredness of hockey, and momentum to take action that has been provided by a male victim.

May:
Four articles, none front page. First two articles focus on James' eligibility for parole by September 1997 (less than eight months after sentencing). Campbell (*Globe and Mail*) raises other issues of abuse such as sexual touching, being forced to play when injured and being insulted.

June and July:
No articles. The Canadian Association for the Advancement of Women and Sport released its summer edition of *Action* and urges readers to get informed about "aspects of sexuality." Puts homosexuality in with STD's, birth control and sexual intercourse—odd choices. Links racial, homophobic and sexist slurs as part of the climate that needs to be changed. Raises the higher vulnerability of girls and of those who have disabilities to sexual abuse.

August:
Four articles, none front page. These are on the heels of the Gordon Kirke report, an organizational response to the situation in hockey. References to James "and his ilk" and the use of cultures as all having light and shadows ... and that they are only now considering their dark secrets (Joyce, *Globe and Mail*). The *Globe and Mail* editorial for Aug. 9 says to stop drafting kids into junior hockey, a point that was ignored by the Kirke report. "These players can be as young as 15 years old and be relocated, by the draft, hundreds of kilometres away from home."

September:
One article addressing the zero-tolerance policy.

October:
No articles. One story on a local radio station in Winnipeg indicated that Graham James charged with indecent assault and gross indecency.

November:
Two articles, none front page. Both are about the Maple Leaf Gardens scandal—no mention of James in either one, surprising. The first is the obituary in "Lives Lived" of Martin Kruze, the outspoken victim of at least two abusers at the Maple Leaf Gardens hockey arena.

December:
One article, Kennedy named Canada's top news maker. Kruze was inspired by Kennedy. The two are linked in the press.

1998–1999
January: Sheldon Kennedy goes on Jane Hawkins Live, a major Canadian talk show
February 28: Four articles, one front page. After seven court dates, one for charges, five for remands, James pleads guilty and is sentenced to six months concurrent for indecent assault. James was eighteen, the player was fourteen. The second charge of gross indecency was stayed because James could not be convicted on both charges. An ex-player had been motivated by Kennedy's courage so he had come forward and pressed charges. Public response is one of dismay and anger at the apparent "non-sentence."
August 9, 1998: Kennedy returns to Moose Jaw to raise awareness about child sexual abuse. This is where much of the abuse occurred (*Globe and Mail*, A7).

October 17, 1998: Jack Batten reviews Laura Robinson's book, *Crossing the Line* (McLelland and Stewart, 1998). Robinson documents a large number of sexual abuse cases in hockey, including the Graham James case.
October 22, 1998: Two articles, one in the *Winnipeg Free Press* (A3) and the other in Globe and Mail (A3), highlight the parole hearing for Graham James. James apologizes to his victims and gets day parole for six months. Full statutory release will be in May, 1999. He is not allowed contact with his victims nor with boys under the age of eighteen years of age. While in jail, James sought sexual counselling, was a model prisoner and is deemed unlikely to reoffend says the parole board. James attributes the sexual abuse to his homosexual tendencies and that he had to "conceal his true nature to succeed in hockey."
December 14, 1998: Kennedy, who is in-line skating across Canada to raise money for child sexual abuse education, draws fire for getting a salary during the project.
December 15, 1998: Two articles, both in the *Globe and Mail* (A27, A7), focus on the Kennedy salary issue and the suit filed by the unnamed victim of James and parents. Being sued are the Western Hockey League, the Swift Current Broncos, the Canadian Hockey League and the Canadian Hockey Association.
Jan. 16, 1999: In the Graham James case, two dozen individuals and businesses are being sued by the second of the sexual abuse victims and his parents. In these claims, the complainants allege that the individuals names and the organizations knew or should have known about the abuse, that the abuse was an open secret (*National Post*, A1).

national team from 1991 to 1996 (Kirby and Greaves 1997). These high performance athletes, representing a wide range of sports, anonymously reported their experiences with sexual abuse and harassment in the sporting context.

Over the past two decades, there have been major trends in understanding and exposing interpersonal violence in Canadian society.[1] The efforts of a large number of survivors, anti-violence activists, treatment providers and researchers have led to growing awareness of the issues of violence, particularly that levelled against women and children. Old patterns of sexual abuse, harassment and sexual assault that had formerly been hidden or denied have been made public. Such efforts have led to government inquiries, a national survey on violence against women and children in Canada, and protocol, policy and legislative changes.

Research and activism have concentrated on making public what were once very private activities: incest, sexual abuse of boys and girls, woman abuse, rape, sexual assault and sexual harassment. In particular, the violence within family and work environments has been scrutinized. In the global context, the anti-violence movement has addressed genital mutilation, female infanticide, sexual slavery and other oppressive practices that violate women and children.

The shift from private to public has been noticeable and dramatic. Practices that were previously secretive and shameful have become publicly deplored and increasingly criminalized. Victims and survivors of sexual abuse, assault and harassment have begun to find avenues for their stories and individually and collectively voice demands for recognition and redress. The growing application of criminal and civil sanctions to such practices has reinforced the "public" aspects of these behaviours and underlined a collective responsibility for providing a safe environment for all.

An increased awareness of the dynamics of violence in relationships and a growing respect for victims' rights to disclose and seek help and compensation have also developed over the past two decades. The collective efforts of the feminist-inspired anti-violence movement, in conjunction with the efforts of committed individuals in the criminal justice system, social services and governments have led to many changes. Legislation and policy development, public and professional education and training, and improvements in procedures and protocols have occurred in many organizations and institutions in efforts to prevent or respond to violence.

Indeed, this process of unveiling the private agony of sexual abuse and harassment has affected most of society's major institutions. Churches have faced exposure of sexual abuse perpetrators within their ranks. Major scandals involving orphanages, church choirs, training schools and clergy have resulted in class and individual actions, compensation packages, public apologies and moral redress.

Schools have had to face similar revelations and deal with the reactions of parents, children and the public. Issues of harassment and abuse perpetrated by teachers and other school board employees on the children under their supervision have caused shock in communities and fear of liability in school boards. Policies regarding corporal punishment in schools have been criticized. The inadequacy of screening and tracking systems of previously convicted teachers has often been brought to light in these circumstances. Training and residential schools, often run by church organizations or governments, have been particularly highlighted as sites of both sexual and physical abuse.

The military has had to deal with several exposures of sexual abuse and manifestations of violence. A confusing mix of the encouragement of violence in the name of war but the expectation of none within the military community or toward civilians is illustrated in these incidents. The public exposure of "hazing" as an initiation rite has fuelled a critique of the violent culture within the military. Reports of sexual and physical violence toward female recruits have received publicity in both Canada and the United States. Sexual and physical violence toward civilians encountered in peacekeeping settings has been particularly embarrassing to the Canadian government.

Another powerful social institution is the media.Television, print, film and the internet have been accused of creating and endorsing violent behaviour in youthful audiences. Although research on the link between violent media imagery and violent behaviour is not fully conclusive, various voluntary codes have been adopted to limit violent imagery, and classification systems have been imposed on producers by agencies and governments. The advertising industry has been held accountable through such mechanisms, sometimes resulting in the retraction of certain campaigns.The Hollywood film industry has been particularly scrutinized of late following several North American incidents of youth carrying out gun-related crimes that are said to copy movie plots. In addition, the linkage between pornography and sexual violence has been much discussed.

The most profound changes, however, have occurred in the family. Traditionally the most private of places and ideally the sanctuary of emotional support and love, the family has been transformed into a site of intense public interest. Physical, emotional and sexual abuse of women and children within family life have become exposed, publicized, analyzed and criminalized. The characterization of these abuses as either private, justifiable or insignificant has been thoroughly rejected in Canadian life.[2]

The institution of sport, in contrast, has been relatively untouched by these trends of the past two decades. For a variety of reasons, sport has evaded the same level of scrutiny and exposure. Brackenridge (1997b:118-19) points out that abuse in sport has been under-researched, inevitably leading to an absence of reliable prevalence rates. Only recently have incidents of sexual and physical abuse finally been brought to light. Articulating this situation and offering unique documentation

of the abuse practices within sport are the voices of the high performance athletes we surveyed in Canada in 1996. Explaining this delay and
analysing these data are the challenges that form the backdrop for this
book.

Explaining the delay in applying the relationship-violence lens to
sport prompts us to assess the ideological underpinnings of sport and
the structure of the sporting context. What are the values that are paramount in the institution of sport and how have they affected disclosure
and scrutiny of sexual abuses within it? How have such values been
dominant enough to supersede and suppress the stories of sport-based
sexual abuse and harassment? How is it that sport has resisted vast
social changes in attitudes and values surrounding sexual abuse in general? As Celia Brackenridge states in our preface (p.11), "recognizing
that sexual abuse occurs in sport requires no more than recognizing
that sport is simply part of society." Why, then, has sport proven so
resistant to the trends in other social institutions? How is sport different or more complicated? What is the place of sport in our culture and
how has this insulated sport from analyses of sexual violence?

Exposing sexual abuse and harassment in sport has now finally begun in earnest. On November 2, 1993, *The Fifth Estate*, a television program of the Canadian Broadcasting Corporation, revealed the story of
a pattern of secretive sexual abuse perpetrated by a coach on some of
his female rowers in Woodstock, Ontario (CBC 1993). In the same program, allusions were also made to a swimming coach abusing one of
his female athletes. The long reaching effects of these experiences on
the young women were plain to see. The perpetuation of denial was
just as plain, not only in the coaches, but also in some of the sport organizations themselves. Mixtures of shock, denial and outrage formed
the reaction among athletes, coaches, parents and sports organization
personnel. It was clear that even in 1993, a full twenty years after the
establishment of the beginnings of the modern phase of the anti-violence movement in Canada, the news that sexual abuse and harassment
existed in sport was almost impossible to accept.

Disclosure can often mean relief and release for victims of such practices, whether they go public or not. It has meant criminal cases, civil
suits and collective action. The use of the legal system can be therapeutic for some but not all and seems to depend strongly on the motivations
of the individual in seeking compensation or making claims (Feldthusen,
Greaves and Hankivsky:2000). Disclosures and suits can provoke policy
changes, procedural shifts and new educational initiatives. However,
they can also lead to ostracism and revictimization. Athletes, particularly those in high performance, competitive, team-based sports, can
(and do) suffer major losses in disclosing such experiences. They stand

Text from "Crossing the Line" (CBC, *The Fifth Estate,* Nov. 2, 1993). Interview by Hana Gartner (HG) with Christine (CC) and Suzanne (SC) (rowers at ages fifteen and seventeen respectively) regarding Doug Clark (rowing coach).

HG ... It started in Woodstock Ontario when a big city rowing coach convinced a group of inexperienced young girls that he could make champion rowers out of them.

CC He led us down a garden path. There was glory, there was medals. There was the Olympics. He put stars in our eyes.

HG Christine's friend Suzanne was also inspired to join the team.

SC He had a vision and it awoke something in many of us that also wanted to do something with our lives but really hadn't found out what.

HG The teenagers who joined up became known as Doug's little girls. Their lives would be dominated by one thing, rowing, and by one man, their coach, Doug Clark. A former Olympic champion rower, then successful stockbroker, Clark was determined that he and his Woodstock girls would make their mark on Canadian rowing. He demanded total dedication, discipline and devotion.

CC We would train in the mornings for a couple of hours. We would train on our lunch hours. We would train for a couple of hours after school. Then you would drag yourself home, eat supper, do your homework for a couple of hours, go to bed, then get up a 4:30 in the morning and you're at it again.

SC You have to be tougher than everybody else or you'll never make it. You'll be a failure in life.

CC It was always flat out until you passed out. And we'd strive to do that. We would work so hard that we'd try to pass out when we worked out.

HG You would abuse yourself physically to get his approval?

CC I didn't look at it as abusing myself. I didn't know any better. He just knew how to plug into each person's mind—differently— whether he'd threaten them or whether he'd hang carrots in front of them. He was the person that we had to trust to get us to our goal. We trusted him.

HG How hungry were you for that goal?

CC Very hungry!

HG So hungry that one year after she started rowing, Christine became Canadian Champion, two years later, a junior World Champion with so many gold medals that she can't even remember them all. Christine was fifteen and on her way out of small-town Ontario and off to the top of international rowing. Christine will never forget the coach who gave her a purpose and an escape from an unhappy family life— Doug Clark.

CC He was a very charismatic man. He was unlike any other man I'd ever met. ... Hm. You know, he swept me away.

HG Had you had boyfriends?

CC Not any serious boyfriends. You know, I was fifteen and I was very vulnerable. I was reaching for somebody who really cared for me. He was the person who cared about me, and so, I fell in love with him. And he said he loved me.

HG Christine believed Doug Clark, and she believed him when he said one day they would be married. and so she found herself being drawn into her first intimate relationship with a man twenty years older than her.

CC It went from an innocent hug after a hard workout or whatever, to eventually kissing and to eventually going far beyond that to ... eventually, I slept with him.

HG What was Doug Clark telling you? Was there a suggestion that the relationship should be kept secret?

CC Yes, there were suggestions that "no one would understand, Christine, this is our secret"?

HG One year after Doug Clark came to town the Woodstock girls rowed their way to gold at the Canadian Championships. They shared success but not their secrets. Christine was not the only girl who was sexually involved with Clark. There were two others. One of them was the girl who rowed next to Christine. Suzanne was seventeen and she too thought her relationship with Clark was the real thing.

SC I was falling in love. It was really important in my life. Yes.

HG Your first love? What was he telling you?

SC He told me all the things that you say to someone that you really loved.

HG You believed you were the only one?

SC Yes, definitely.

HG Clark went out of his way to spend time alone with Suzanne. He would visit her when she babysat and took her for drives in the countryside after practice. Suzanne who had never even kissed a boy before remembers ....

SC Well, all the physical intimacy, that kissing, hugging, that touching—not just at the shoulder or at the knee—all that sexual intimacy. I didn't go have sexual intercourse with him but it went a long way beyond any kind of friendship.

HG Christine also spent many evenings alone with Doug Clark. Once when she was seventeen years old, she refused to be intimate with him. Furious, he drove her the five miles back to her house without a word.

CC I was so angry with him that I got out of the car and slammed the door as hard as I could. And then he rolled down his window and said, "Don't you ever do that again!" So I stormed into my house and I just had immense fear all night long because I thought "Oh, gosh. He'll never let me row again." So, the next morning, I woke before anyone else and I rode my bike all the way out to his house and I apologized.

HG Your rode ten miles on your bicycle to apologize because you did not want to be intimate with him that night?

CC Yes, That's the kind of power that he had.

On other occasions, you know, he would say to me, "I can replace you ... Do you want me to move so and so up into your seat?" and I'd say "no, of course not" ... "Well then" (he'd say).

HG Clark encouraged intense competition amongst the girls for places in the boat. Suzanne says that he even pitted her and her two sisters, Heather and Tina, against each other. So Suzanne didn't share her secrets with her sisters, and she couldn't tell her mother, who was seriously ill with cancer.

SC She could tell that there was some unusual feelings, that I was very attached to him, and she asked me, and I just thought "I can't tell her ... I can't admit that."

HG Why?

SC She died just after I turned eighteen and the beginning of my grade-thirteen year, and she was dying, and it was a long slow process, so, no, I couldn't tell her.

HG The girls kept silent for over fifteen years. Only recently have they found out about each other's relationship with coach Clark. Clark left Woodstock in 1980 and went to the top of Canadian coaching. Five years ago (1988), he returned to the business world. He declined our invitation to an interview and denied ever having had a sexual relationship with any of the young women on the Woodstock rowing club. Suzanne claims her relationship with Clark lasted two years. Christine says she was involved with Clark for almost six years. Both thought they were the only one. Each thought he would marry them. Clark did make them champions but Christine believes the price they paid was too high.

CC It was so wrong to do ... to violate somebody's psyche and emotions to that extent ... for the pure goal of achievement.

SC I felt like a special person and never really saw ... I never really realized ... that it was just talk. That it was all to get what he really wanted.

CC I don't know what I would ever say to him if I met him. I don't. I think in one case I would hug him and then I would slap him as hard as I could, because of my anger.

HG Why would you hug him? You don't still love him, do you?

CC No, no ... I think, it's, um ... because I gained a lot out of rowing and I achieved a lot and that really came through him and ....

HG So why are you crying?

CC For a man that I had such great respect for and loyalty, to find out afterwards, all the things he really did do. It was just one big case of deception. And I was a sucker to fall for it. A lot of us were.

to lose their place on the team, the support of their teammates, their career path, their friends and their "family." They may find themselves cut off from the activity they most love, their sport. Understanding these elements of the sport culture and their impact on both disclosure and reaction is the purview of this book.

The dynamics of interpersonal violence are now well known. Happening within a relationship of some sort, whether familial, custodial, authoritative or employment-related, sexual abuse and sexual harassment have a profound effect on the victim. Often such abuse is systematic and patterned, and may often be long-term. It is usually conducted in isolation, and it isolates the victim from her/his peers. Secrecy is usually a required ingredient for maintaining this isolation. Without fail, there is an unequal distribution of power between the perpetrator and the victim(s). There is often an explicit or implicit threat regarding disclosure, suggesting (unfortunately correctly) that the victim will lose something valuable if the abuse comes to light.

There are often contradictory feelings and emotions regarding the perpetrator and the abuse and its meaning. Mixtures of loyalty, commitment, fealty, affection, guilt and shame contribute to denial and work against disclosure. Often, the perpetrators misuse their authority or assume power over their victims. The perpetrator may exploit the vulnerabilities or the wish of the child or adult for love, harmony and emotional support. Such complexity can only increase the damage of such relationships, sentencing the victim to lifelong social, psychological and economic reverberations. These features of relationship violence are well known after twenty-five years of study and activism (see Herman 1992).

Applying this knowledge to the institution of sport and sporting situations is crucial. Brackenridge offers a model whereby she identifies many characteristics that add a sport-specific layer of risk factors to our understanding of sexual abuse (1997b:126). Included in this list are opportunities and expectations of physical contact during the training and coaching exchange in sport, opportunities for extended trips or training camp sessions, and a poor climate for debating sexual abuse and developing sport-wide responses to it. Overarching these practical aspects, however, are the values and goals of the sport enterprise. These influences overlap and encircle the experiences and relationships of the athlete and the team. These are the values of sport. As Brackenridge (1997b:127) points out, sexual abuse in sport is among a range of issues that can be sidelined by overriding values such as achieving results and winning.

Several values appear to have a huge impact on sport. Building physical skill and prowess is seen as equivalent to health and has often been perceived as morally good. Despite the fact that extreme training can often compromise health, the notion of linking sport, health and goodness persists. The liberation of the human body in sport, as manifested in the notion that athletes have supreme control over their bodies, is very much at odds with the serious loss of control involved in being sexually abused or sexually harassed. As a result, a complex rejigging of self and identity is required to absorb the experience of abuse in the sport context.

A second overriding value of sport is its foundation on a male model. Despite increased opportunity for girls and women in sport, it remains a male domain, reflective of its setting in a patriarchal society. Not surprisingly, the female experience of sport cultures is often a replication of societal gendered power relations (Tomlinson and Yorganci 1997:135; Gagnon 1997:66). Indications of this are its gendered inequality in resource allocation and the male domination of coaching and training. Sports themselves are organized along gender lines, with activities designated for one or the other sex. More critically, for the analysis of abuse within sport, it is a site of creating the male and defining masculinity. Men who succeed in sport are granted extremely high status and prestige. This sets the stage for the use of power as a way to control others, the absolute underpinning of interpersonal violence. As Lenskyj (1992b:22) points out, this can manifest as outright misogyny and can serve to protect athletes from being called on poor or criminal behaviour. This protection is often in the name of ensuring the high performance and good reputation of the team and its sponsors. Tomlinson and Yorganci (1997:136) also argue that the gendered power relations inherent in sport lead to sexual abuse.

As well, sport is dominated by a heterosexual model. For women and girls in sport, success often includes sexual attractiveness, sexual suggestiveness and conformity to a heterosexual image of femininity. Sports such as gymnastics, ice skating and synchronized swimming illustrate these influences in their content, judging, costumery and presentation. Somehow, for females, the strength and endurance required to be a high performance athlete needs tempering by exploitative sexual images. This contributes to a sexually charged atmosphere, where sexual measures of success are not too remote from the everyday reality of the sport, in training and competition. While sexual abuse is about power, not sexual activity, when sexual measures become part of the scale of success, trainers and coaches and judges will push to develop these aspects of the athletes under their influence. The heterosexual value overlaid on sport also leads to homophobic harassment (Lenskyj 1992b:27); thus an additional layer of silence exists for athletes, coaches and trainers alike who are lesbian or gay.

Another strong value stems from the importance of sport to the country. It evokes and contributes to patriotism and the building of the national identity. This comes into focus when high performance athletes represent their home country or national group in competition. If a country becomes very proud of an athlete the rewards are strong. This kind of power and prestige can contribute to insulating the athlete from the effects of being either a perpetrator or a victim of sexual abuse. The disclosure or accusation of sexual abuse lies in deep contradiction to the patriotism and pride attached to athletic performance.

One of the most powerful values overlaying sport is that of the loyalty attached to the family-like structures in sport. Familism dominates sporting training and practice. Its impact can be seen in the attachment and cohesion inspired by the structures in team sports. Crucial emotional needs are met in the crucible of the team—it becomes the primary group for an individual, providing a context for love, loyalty and identity, needs that are usually met in the family of origin, or, for adults, in the created family. In high performance sport, team members are explicitly encouraged to commit themselves to the shared goals of the team, to their teammates and to their coaches and trainers. The team becomes their family. Sometimes, athletes are young and impressionable when they join the team and are separated from their own families. The coach can function as the "head of the family," the teammates as siblings and the ancillary personnel as cousins and extended family. This creates a context of a code of silence that works against disclosures, a perfect environment for systematic sexual abuse.

Structurally, high performance sport is essentially an unregulated workplace where athletes are expected to devote themselves to the goal and to demonstrate a strong work ethic. Yet they remain ill-protected by regulations, laws and policies that normally offer workers rights and avenues of redress. This disempowering structure sets the stage for exploitation and silence. If and when sexual abuse occurs, the structure does not assist the athlete in speaking out, seeking redress or righting situations.

These values are laced together and projected onto the public screen, creating an image of sport that is a powerful and important reflection of the culture. In the media, sport becomes noticeable when things go badly or well, when winning or record-breaking takes place, or when scandals or disasters strike. The media can control the release of information about sexual abuse and harassment, or they can simply create a domain where it is hard to talk about. Either way, the media must be dealt with in disclosure and implicated in silence.

The image of sport is one of a clean and safe activity. There is an element of moral hygiene and "clean-living" which counters the easy understanding of sport as a site of sexual abuse or harassment. The dedication required to become a high performance athlete contributes to this image—developing and taking care of the body are seen as activities that require an enormous amount of commitment, perseverance and concentrated focus. That athletes do this voluntarily and many with minimum financial support or reward adds to the mystique. The assumption is that those coaching and supporting the athlete are also highly committed and dedicated individuals. Sport organizations, the next element in the sport structure, are as well strongly associated with high moral values and upstanding organizational goals.

All of these assumptions counter the disclosure of sexual abuse by victims or witnesses, effective and speedy responses from sport organizations, and the development of policy and protocol in line with other social institutions. But these assumptions about moral value are not enough to explain the delay in focusing on sport as a site of sexual abuse and harassment. After all, the church is also perceived to be a place of moral safety, holiness and cleanliness. It is also considered to be a haven, and indeed, to have certain structures and qualities of a family. Why did these moral images of the church not continue to protect it from exposure and disclosure of sexual abuse and harassment? How did the reverence inspired for the mission of the church not continue to insulate it from damage? Is the pressure of spiritual conformity not as great as team conformity? Why has the anti-individualism inherent in both institutions not functioned at similar speeds?

The answer may be that the elements described above add up to encase the issue of sexual abuse in sport in a very private place. Team athletes are volunteers, focused on a common goal in a highly competitive atmosphere, interdependent on each other and their coaches, and engaged in a highly symbolic, nationally (and locally) valued activity. All of these elements help to form the webbing for the dome of silence that has hung over sport. The reluctance to expose sexual abuse in sport may have been due to the power of such exposure to destroy personal, team or even national identities. Exposing this issue is confusing and highly threatening, similar to revelations of incest in family life. As Brackenridge reports, once the team becomes the surrogate family, sexual abuse by a coach is equated to "virtual incest" (1997b:118). Together, these elements and dynamics would deter the strongest of victims and witnesses. Sport organizations, particularly high performance national teams, are sensitive to any form of scandal that threatens the image of wholesomeness, health and moral superiority of sport. Charges of sexual harassment and abuse compromise the prospect of team members being considered fine ambassadors and examples of patriotic citizenship. Whether the scandal is about sexual abuse, drug use or embezzlement, the sport establishment in Canada has been acutely aware of its public image and has reacted negatively to such tribulations. All of these tensions surround the phenomenon of sexual abuse and sexual harassment in sport, and they all help suppress disclosure and exposure. This may help to account for the resistance, until the 1990s, of the sport institution to the floodlight of analysis that has been applied to the church, the school and the family in the last twenty-five years. Most important, they may help us understand the athletes' experiences and their collective silence, until now.

The athletes' own words help us fill in some of this picture. The data from the national survey reported here are the first illumination of the prevalence of sexual abuse and harassment in high performance team settings. These words point to a clear need for a redefinition of sport and a clarification of values attached to the sporting enterprise. Finally, and most difficult, there is a need for sport organizations, the public and governments to develop policies and protocol that reflect ethically sound sporting practice and that protect athletes and illuminate sport. Changing the values of sport requires a reassessment of the values of the society which supports it. Are we collectively interested in returning sport to the athlete, in making sport safe and in rewarding honesty and transparency? Are we ready to retract the dome?

Chapter Two describes the methodology and results of a survey undertaken in 1996 in Canada. All of the national-team members, both male and female, were asked a wide range of questions regarding their experiences, knowledge and understanding of sexual abuse and harassment in the sport context. The survey elicited both quantitative and qualitative data. The athletes were asked to give details on one incident which they found particularly upsetting. The survey did not collect data on the duration or frequency of abuse encountered by the athletes in the sport context nor on the experiences of abuse outside of that context. Definitions of abuse and harassment were provided to ensure clarity of response.

Some key findings from the 266 respondents (55 percent female, 45 percent male) indicate that a significant portion (40 percent) of the athletes felt that sexual abuse, harassment and assault were definite issues in sport. Not surprisingly, females felt more at risk and consequently more vulnerable to sexual abuse, assault and harassment than the male athletes (86 percent to 14 percent), although male respondents felt more fear about the potential for child sexual abuse in sport. Coaches were the most likely to be identified as the perpetrators of sexual abuse, harassment or assault in the incidents recollected by the respondents. Social and physical isolation was a key feature of many of the incidents relayed, a feature which made the athlete more vulnerable to both the assaults or abuses and less likely to disclose. Many of these incidents were framed in "relationships" that lasted over extended periods of time, and many went unreported. Thus, relationships based on trust and familiarity between athlete and coach were often violated and the violations then kept secret. The most frequent location for these incidents was team trips. Both different-sex and same-sex harassment and abuse featured in the reports from the athletes.

In short, the issues of abuse, assault and harassment were of concern to the athletes, unreported and gendered. They occurred in a chilly, often homophobic climate. They ranged from verbal sexual abuse to sexual assault to rape. They included child sexual assault in five cases, where athletes reported that they had been subjected to forced sexual intercourse prior to age sixteen, most often by someone more than twenty years older than them. Of the few who lodged complaints about incidents of abuse, few of those were satisfied with the outcome. In all, the evidence from this survey shows the need for fuller and more effective mechanisms for prevention and redress.

Chapter Three looks in detail at the values and imperatives of sport. The values articulated above are grouped under seven headings and described as "imperatives" that drive the very foundation of sport as an institution. While many aspects of these imperatives can be positive (e.g., competition, the work ethic, nationalism, etc.), it is the negative or contradictory elements that we investigate in detail. It is the potential of these imperatives to create or foster negative situations that, we argue, can compromise sport by limiting and contorting the sport experience. Parallel to this, the sport institution and its organizations develop defences and reactions to negative events within sport that further compromise the institution. It is in this complex web of values and imperatives that the potential for violence against athletes has taken root, evaded scrutiny and avoided exposure. Lastly, these negative values stand in stark contrast to the intended values of sport: its goodness and healthiness, its celebration and liberation of the body.

Chapter Four develops a sport "ethic of care," which is morally based and goes beyond the notions of rule-setting and sanctioning transgressions. While policies and codes of conduct are increasingly common and welcomed by sport organizations and the public, they do not address or guarantee that behaviour in the sport world will be rooted in a set of positive, shared values. Rather, they often focus on catching rule-breakers and/or avoiding liability. While it will be an ongoing challenge in sport to develop a positive ethic of care, we argue that sport is ripe for an advanced application of such principles as equity and athlete-centredness. A deliberate and sport specific ethic of care can be developed that is contextualized in sport, informed by sporting practice, responsive to athletes' rights and concerned about consequences.

Finally in Chapter Five, we discuss what it may take to "retract the dome" of silence over sexual abuse, harassment and assault in sport. While it will not be an easy task, we suggest a mix of actions and policies embedded in a clear "ethic of care" framework that would not only serve athletes better but also transform the institution of sport into a morally sound, fair and liberatory experience of which all could be proud. While this transformation will be a long-term process, some immediate practical questions are also tackled. What protocols, policies and legal responsibilities can be outlined to immediately protect the athletes and open the issues up for scrutiny? How can the shift from private agony to public exposure be encouraged?

We also see some obstacles to retracting the dome. The imperatives named in Chapter Three are powerful and will not be released and replaced easily. In particular, the excising of violence in all of its forms from sport will take some time. The task of shifting sport organizations from a liability and risk-aversion position to an athlete-centred position will take vision and resources. Ensuring the provision of safety, particularly for female athletes, in a continuing context of inequitable sport, will be demanding. However, the true test of the institution of sport will be in its speed and willingness to make these changes, to transform denial and resistance into action and caring.

NOTES

1. For example, Statistics Canada's 1993 violence against women survey was the first study internationally to document adult experiences with sexual and physical assault by marital partners, dates and boyfriends, other men known to women, and strangers. It reported:
    - One-half of all Canadian women had experienced at least one incident of violence since the age of sixteen.
    - Almost one-half of women reported violence by men known to them and one-quarter reported violence by a stranger.
    - One quarter of all women had experienced violence at the hands of a current or past marital partner (includes common-law unions).
    - One in six currently married women reported violence by their spouses;

one-half of women with previous marriages reported violence by a previous spouse.

- More than one in ten women who reported violence in a current marriage had at some point felt their lives were in danger.
- Six in ten Canadian women who walk alone in their own area after dark feel "very" or "somewhat" worried doing so.
- Women with violent fathers-in-law are at three times the risk of assault by their partners than are women with non-violent fathers-in-law. (Statistics Canada 1993)

2. This whole process has not been easy. The pressures to keep silent have often been intense within families, and until recently, little public understanding has been available to victims of family violence. The confounding context of love and security, contaminated by violence and abuse, has deterred many from disclosure. Even with disclosure, the spectre of revictimization by the perpetrator or "the system" has loomed large.

Chapter Two

The Nature and Scope of the Problem amongst Canada's High Performance Athletes

Paul Hickson article (from *The Observer* **website, Sept. 27, 1995, United Kingdon)**
Paul Hickson, Britain's head swimming coach at the Seoul Olympics, was jailed for 17 years Wednesday for raping two women and indecently assaulting 13 while coaching them at school and college.

Hickson, 48, whose 1988 Olympic swimming team captured three golds plus silver and bronze medals, was said to have committed a catalogue of sex attacks spread over a 15-year period while he ran swimming clubs in Norwich, England, and Swansea, Wales, before he became national coach.

One women, now 32, described how Hickson frequently raped her at his home during school lunch breaks—the first time when she was "13.

"It is a terrible shame to see a man of your great ability in the dock at all," judge John Prosser said before passing sentence.

"You enjoyed, until the time of your arrest, national and international veneration in the swimming world. Your efforts brought out the best potential

Our research[1] confirms that sexual abuse of high performance athletes, particularly female athletes, is a major problem in Canadian sport. Sexual abuse has been a problem in sport for many years but has only recently come to the public's attention through Canadian criminal cases such as those of Graham James, a junior hockey coach in Swift Current, Saskatchewan, and Graham Smith, an Edmonton track and field coach. On January 2, 1997, Graham James received a sentence of three and a half years for sexual assaults over a number of years against two young male hockey players in his charge. One year later, on January 27, 1998, he received a six-month sentence to be served concurrently with two earlier sentences for sexual offences. In 1993, Graham Smith was jailed for two and a half years for sexually assaulting young female athletes. Criminal charges have also been laid in the United Kingdom, for example, in the 1994 case of Paul Hickson, a national swimming coach. Hickson received a seventeen-year sentence for sexual assaults against young female swimmers in his care (Brackenridge et al. 1995). In another case, one where charges could not be laid, Thomas Hamilton killed himself after shooting to death fourteen school children and one teacher at Dunblane School in Scotland in March of 1996.[2] Through volunteering in a variety of sports clubs, Hamilton had gained access to numerous children. Revelations in 1996 of a possible pedophile ring operating at Maple Leaf Garin some of our greatest swimmers and they looked up to you." Hickson denied two charges of rape and 13 indecent assaults. Married with an 8-year-old daughter, he accused the 13 women of fantasizing about sex with him.

dens in Toronto in connection with hockey games have represented one more shock wave to sport organizations and to the public (*Globe and Mail*, Feb.–March, 1997). In all these cases, the abusers or perpetrators used sport for sexual access to children.

Though sexual harassment and abuse problems have long been both pervasive and serious in sport, athletes seldom lay complaints against their abusers. The lack of formal complaints may lead those in sport to believe the problem is minor or that it only occurs amongst sport people unknown to them. However, "denial of the possibility of sexual abuse in sport has recently started to break down in the face of a number of major legal cases against prominent national and international level coaches" (Brackenridge 1996b:3). We have found the problem to be a large one indeed, affecting participants at virtually all levels of sport.

Other researchers have also turned their attention to sexual harassment and abuse in sport, starting with the work of Brackenridge in England (1987, 1990, 1996b, 1997a, 1997b, 1997c; Brackenridge and Kirby 1997). Also, important research exists in the U.S. by Pike-Masteralexis (1995) and Volkwein (1996); in Norway (Fasting 1999), and in Canada by researchers such as Donnelly, Casperson, Sergeant and Steenhof (1993), Kirby (1995), Kirby and Greaves (1997) Brackenridge and Kirby (1999) and Lenskyj (1992a, 1992b, 1994). To this point, there have been no extensive studies in Canada about abuse in particular sports. Although studies outside of sport indicate the kind of sexual violence experienced by women and children, these have not specifically addressed the sexual harassment and abuse which occurs to both females and males within the sport context (Canadian Panel on Violence Against Women 1993). As governments and sport organizations seek to develop preventative measures, it is important that the nature and scope of the problem of sexual harassment and abuse in sport be thoroughly understood.

The data in this chapter are the first on the type and pervasiveness of sexual harassment and abuse problems reported by high performance and recently retired athletes in Canada, indeed in the world. However, other Canadian studies do exist which look specifically at sexual harassment in university sport and physical education (Lenskyj 1992b; Holman 1995), discrimination against athletes on the basis of sexual orientation (Fusco 1995; Fusco and Kirby 2000) or on the basis of race (Paraschak 1990) and violence in sport (Pronger 1993).

With the financial assistance of Sport Canada,[3] a Canada-wide survey of sexual harassment and abuse of national-team athletes was completed in mid-1996. The bilingual survey questioned athletes' awareness of the issues, experiences of sexual harassment and abuse and thoughts about how sexual abuse could be eradicated from sport. The role of Athletes CAN, the association for Canada's elite athletes, was critical to the success of the study for it enabled us to guarantee confidentiality and anonymity even to the best known Canadian athletes. All questions about sexual harassment and abuse were about the context of sport. Included in this chapter are the results from 266 completed surveys.

The definitions we used are perhaps the most controversial part of the study. The sexual activities included in each of these terms vary across jurisdictions and in everyday usage. Numerous terms for sexual abuse exist, among them: sexual harassment, chilly climate (Lenskyj 1994); sexual assault, sexual predation (Canadian Council for Ethics in Sport 1997); sexual exploitation and grooming (Gonsiorek 1995; Brackenridge 1996b); sexual exploitation, pornography, prostitution and trafficking (Kelly et al. 1995). There are also terms for the kinds of sexual abuse which occur within families. These include incest, child abuse, child sexual abuse, wife abuse and family violence. Our research is further complicated by difficulty in defining who is a child, a young person or an adult across various jurisdictions as laws defining these terms vary from country to country. And, as if that is not difficult enough, we are also faced with a plethora of terms for the perpetrators of abuse. They may be named as any combination of the following: sexual abusers, sexual harassers, sexual molesters, sexual predators, pedophiles, sexual exploiters, child traffickers and pornographers (Brackenridge 1997a; Brackenridge and Kirby 1999; Gonsiorek 1995). Kelly et al. (1995) write that there are grounds for both consensus and disagreement in legal, policy, media, organizational and individual uses of these definitions (1997b:5).

For our study, we chose straightforward definitions, ones we thought could be easily understood by all national-team members. As quoted from the survey:

> *Sexual Harassment* is defined as a form of sexual abuse—sexual behaviour that is unwanted or any sexual solicitation or advance directed at an individual/group by another individual/group of the same or opposite sex who knows (or ought to know) the attention is unwanted and is an abuse of power. Often the harasser is someone in a position of authority and is potentially exploitive.
>
> *Sexual Abuse* is defined as any sexual activity performed against the wishes and consent of the victim. It includes being forced to engage in unwanted sex and to participate in unpleasant, vio-

lent or frightening sexual acts. You can be sexually assaulted without being touched. If you've been forced to watch sexual acts, movies or videos, or read pornographic magazines, that's sexual abuse. If someone continually refuses to respect your privacy while you're dressing or when you're in the bathroom, that is also sexual abuse.

Sexual Assault/Rape is defined as a violent crime of power in which sexual activity is used as a weapon. Sexual assault/rape is an intentional, violent act of forced sexual activity—whether it is committed by a stranger or a known and trusted person.

We included examples with the definitions to help athletes describe their experiences. We avoided legal language. Too wide a variety of definitions from which to choose could be overwhelming[4] and the ones we chose are easily understandable, in fairly common usage and allow other researchers to do some comparative studies.

How We Analyzed the Surveys

We used two steps, one quantitative and the other, qualitative. What we present here are both the statistical findings and qualitative information provided by participating athletes about sexual violence they have seen or heard about or experienced within the context of sport.[5] We must point out that athletes were asked to describe only the sexual harassment or abuse experience which upset them the most. This means we can count the number of athletes reporting a particular form of harassment or abuse but not whether they experienced it more than once. There is a built-in form of under reporting in this, a cross-sectional measure of the nature and scope of sexual harassment and abuse. Another measure of under-reporting is that we sought no information on the duration, frequency or number of abusers involved in the abuse. Further, because athletes are describing the experience which upset them the most, it is not necessarily the most serious in terms of interpretation by the law or in long-term consequences for the athlete. Since we wanted to establish a baseline of data, we were looking for collective or group patterns. Individual sexual harassment and abuse profiles are unavailable even though athletes may have provided enough information for us to compile these. To protect the identity of these high profile athletes, we removed all context specific and personally identifying information. While the profiles may, in the long run, have proved useful to understanding the particular dynamics of sexual violence, we did not consider this within our mandate. Overall, we have determined the scope of the problem from the athletes' perspective, but have only the "tip of the iceberg" in terms of the nature, severity and frequency with which individual athletes experience sexual violence. This does not allow us to comment on the frequency with which particular athletes experience sexual predation over a period of time but does provide us with a conservatively interpreted set of data with which to work.

We wish to point out two additional caveats. First, the results included in this chapter do not represent the full scope of the problem of sexual abuse for athletes. Our figures indicate high levels of sexual harassment and abuse but they certainly do not account for all the sexual harassment and abuse these athletes may have experienced. While other research suggests that there may be a relationship between sexual abuse outside the context of sport and that experienced in the sporting context (Brackenridge 1997c), we did not ask about abuse athletes may have experienced outside of sport, nor, as stated above, can we report on how frequently particular forms of harassment or abuse of athletes occur within a particular sport. This means that our figures under-represent, in a major way, the actual frequency of athlete abuse. Second, we did not ask whether the athletes were perpetrators of harassment and abuse. Given these factors, our results represent only an initial determination of the types and prevalence of sexual harassment and abuse in sport.

We report the results in four sections paralleling the original survey: athlete characteristics, awareness of the issues, what has been seen or heard, and personal harassment and abuse experiences and perceptions.

Athlete Characteristics
A typical athlete responding to the 1996 survey is one who is currently on a national team and has been for more than five years, averages twenty-five years of age, is probably unmarried with no children, has lived with his/her parents throughout the majority of the competitive years and has a total personal annual income of approximately $10,000 (salaries quoted in this research are in Canadian dollars). This athlete has most likely achieved at least college graduation and is a full-time athlete who also works or attends school full-time. She or he is most likely Caucasian, English-speaking and has had a male coach throughout their national-team experience.

Sex
More females than males responded, 55.6 percent to 44.4 percent. This is an unusual figure given that females, on average, occupy only 30 to 35 percent of international, multi-sport teams.[6] This may mean females are more concerned about sexual harassment issues than are males and/or that males generally think of sexual harassment as behaviour which

Figure 1: General Description of Respondents

Sex	Female 55.6%	Male 44.6%
	Active 55%	Active 58%
	Retired 45	Retired 42%
Age	Average 25.8 years	Range 14–60 years
Years on Team	Average 5.38 years	Range 1–20 years
Residence	Urban 41%	Suburban/rural 59%
Relationship Status	Single/Alone 50%	Married 38% Other 9%
Have Children	Yes 11.3%	No 88.7%
Work *	Full-time	Part-time
	Athlete 48%	Athlete 33%
	Paid work 25.2%	Paid work 14.7%
	Student 32%	Student NR
Income	Average $10,000	Range $0–$50,000+
Education **	High School or Less 38%	College or University Degree 52%
Race/Ethnicity	Caucasian 85%	All Others 15%
Preferred Language	English 76%	French 21% Other 3%
Disability Status	Yes 15%	No 85%
Sexually Active	Female average	Male average
at What Age ***	= 18 years	= 16.5 years

* *Includes 13.9% of respondents who consider themselves to be both full-time athletes and students.*

** *7.3% of respondents are less than 18 years of age. Many athletes have not yet finished their formal education.*

****Note that this research includes a number of athletes who are still under the reported average ages.*

primarily concerns women. Alternatively, it could indicate a general reluctance among males to discuss or reveal abuse, due to homophobia or shame.

Active or Retired and Geographic Location

In addition to the information in Figure 1 on sex and gender, we also found that most, three-quarters of the athletes who responded, are current members of national teams, 55 percent of them female. Amongst the other quarter, the retired athletes, 59 percent are female (p.<000). Most have been on national teams for many years, averaging 5.38 years with a range of from 1 to 20 years. Since the most frequent response was 3 years, this indicates what in statistics is called a positive skew, that is, that there are a large number of athletes grouped in the 1-to-3-year time and then the rest of the athletes are strung out with diminishing frequency from 3 to 20 years. This means that once athletes are on the national team for 3 years, they are likely to remain on the team for a long period of time.

We were particularly interested in information from recently retired athletes. After all, they could recount, through the full span of an athletic career, whether there had been incidents of sexual predation they have heard about, seen or experienced themselves. In addition, many said that they had more freedom to speak about problems only after they retire (Kirby 1986), because they had little fear of repercussions from the athletic establishment or their peers. It may be that to speak about problems such as sexual abuse before retiring, even within the strict protective structures of an anonymous and confidential survey, would seem risky to some of the currently active athletes.

We found that most elite athletes live in suburban or rural areas. In fact, 4 in 10 reside in urban areas. However, these athletes live all across Canada in a way roughly reflective of the Canadian population, with 27 percent and 22 percent coming from Canada's two most populous provinces, Ontario and Quebec respectively. Responses were received from all provinces and territories except Prince Edward Island. This suggests a good survey distribution method and perhaps also that there is a generalized concern amongst athletes, regardless of location, about sexual predation.

Age and Relationship Status
The athletes responding to the survey ranged in age from 14 to 60 years, and averaged 25.8 years of age. They report "leaving home" at 18.9 years of age although some left home as early as 11 and others as late as age 32. Fully half of the athletes are neither married nor cohabiting. Thirty-eight percent are married or cohabiting while 9 percent report "other" relationship statuses. Only 11.3 percent of respondents have children.

Economics
Athletes are, by and large, relatively poor, and only 1 in 5 had someone economically dependent upon them, a not unexpected result since the majority are still competing and financial payment and sponsorship have been minimal in Canada. Half of the athletes earn less than $10,000 per year. On the other end of the scale, 7.2 percent make $50,000 or more. As expected, the retired athletes in the sample account for a greater number of the higher salaries. [7] This suggests that athletes, even the very successful ones, are not in sport because of its financial rewards. Instead, we picture talented people training and competing in a sport despite the financial hardships of such a life. The stereotype of a high performance athlete as having numerous sponsorships and financial independence certainly does not fit the average national-team athlete.

Education

Even though many of the responding athletes still attend school or university, athletes are a very well educated group. The average level of education in Canada is the completion of high school.[8] Only 38 percent of athletes, many still under eighteen years of age, have educational attainments at or below the Canadian average. More than half have already achieved college or university degrees (e.g., B.A., B.Sc., Law, Medicine) or graduate degrees (M.A., Ph.D.).

This educational attainment can be explained a number of ways. Athletes are regarded as a very motivated group and, in all probability, apply themselves both inside and outside of sport. Also, educational institutes play a major role in supporting student athletes. These institutions may provide athletes with scholarships and bursaries, access to training facilities, medical support, and/or high performance coaches in their disciplines. Sport Canada endorses such support through its Athlete Assistance Program, which includes specific support to qualifying athletes in school. However, not all athletes can benefit from remaining in school. Although the competitive schedules of summer athletes generally fit well with the teaching and examination schedules of institutions of higher learning, the same cannot be said for winter sport athletes. Many of these take lighter course loads because their competitive season occurs in the fall or winter semesters. Despite this, school seems to be a good place for someone training for a national team. Given these supports, many athletes are encouraged and receive opportunities to achieve higher education through their commitment to sport.

Full-time or Part-time Work

Athletes are hard workers both in and out of sport. They may define themselves as athletes or workers or students or some combination of these. Four of every 5 athletes consider themselves to be full- or part-time athletes. These same athletes however, also work for wages: 25.2 percent full-time, 14.7 percent part-time and 6 percent self-employed. One third of athletes also call themselves full-time students. Some athletes (13.9 percent) said that they were employed full-time and were also full-time athletes. This information, combined with the economic and educational factors, means that many athletes combine education and sport training with as much paid work as is feasible. This may be to make financial ends meet and/or to keep some semblance of work/career planning in place. Most of these athletes appear to arrange their work lives around sport's competitive demands.

Racial/ethnic and Linguistic Background
The survey questions on racial/ethnic and linguistic background can only be used as imprecise indicators. Although the racial/ethnic data shows considerable overlaps because athletes could write-in their responses, we do know the following:

1. 85 percent of the athletes are Caucasian,
2. 15 percent are either "Native," "Asian," "African," Mixed Race" or Québécois,
3. 94.7 percent of the athletes were born in Canada.

Similar to Canadian demographics, which indicate that 1 in 4 Canadians has French as a mother tongue, 76 percent of the athletes indicate a preference for communicating in English and 21 percent a preference in French. Three percent are fully bilingual.

Disability Status
Surprisingly, 40 of 266 respondents (15 percent) identify a permanent disability or medical condition. We wanted to know whether athletes were on the so-called "special teams," such as the Canadian Paralympic Team. However, a number of athletes also appeared to use the survey to indicate that they sustained acute or chronic injuries through sport.

Sexual Activity
We asked the athletes at what age they became sexually active and with whom.[9] Are elite athletes, by and large, a sexually active or inactive group? According to our information, athletes become sexually active at roughly the same ages as other members of Canadian society. The average age for female athletes is 18 years of age compared to 16.5 years of age for males. Further, 80.4 percent of females and 90.6 percent of males are sexually active while they are high performance athletes. It appears that both age and income are good predictors of sexual activity. The older the athlete and the lower the income, the more likely the athlete is to be sexually involved with only one person. It may also be that the lower income athletes become sexually active at younger ages.[10] Additionally, most athletes are sexually active within the sporting context, with athletes on the same team (45.4 percent), with athletes on other teams (51.5 percent) or with a coach (2.3 percent).[11]

Sex of Coach
During the majority of the time an athlete was on the national team, they were coached primarily by a female (10 percent), a male (75 percent) or both (14 percent). Sixty percent of the athletes under 16 years of

Table 1: Are High Performance Athletes Sexually Active?

Age at Which Athletes Report Being Sexually Active		
	Female Athletes	*Male Athletes*
Under 16 years	11	16
16–21 years	56	65
22–27 years	8	3
Over 27 years	1	0
Not Reported	14	11

Figure 2: Percentage of Coaches by Age of Athletes

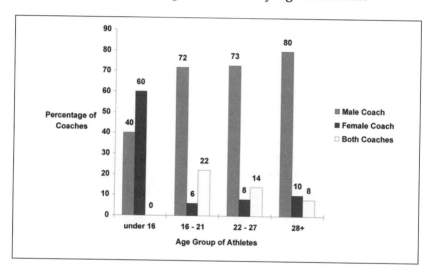

age are coached by females and 40 percent by males. However, as athletes grow older, their chances of being coached by males gradually increased to 72 percent for 16 to 21 year olds, 73.2 percent for 22 to 27 year olds and 80.2 percent for those 28 years of age or older. The chances of being coached by females decreases with equal rapidity.

Coaching is a male-dominated profession at the national-team level. When comparing coaches and gender of athletes, a disturbing but confirmatory picture emerges.

Table 2: Gender of Athlete vs Gender of National-team Coach

	Female Coach	Male Coach	Both
Female athletes	16.5%	65.5%	16.9%
Male athletes	1.7%	87.2%	11.1%

Ninety-three percent of all male athletes and 83.8 percent of female athletes are coached by either males or both females and males. Fewer than 1 in 5 female athletes has consistent exposure to female coaching while they are high performance athletes (p.<000). Clearly, coaching at the high performance level is primarily a male experience.

The preponderance of male coaches corroborates the work of Lenskyj (1986) and Kirby and LeRougetel (1992) which asserts that the majority of athletes experience sport in a male-defined and male-dominated manner. In some countries, there is concern about the absence of female coaches as role models for female (and male) athletes at all levels of sport and the undesirability of the great majority of national-team coaches being male (Kirby and LeRougetel 1992, International Professional Development Program Tour 1993). Our figures add weight to those concerns.

AWARENESS OF THE ISSUE OF SEXUAL HARASSMENT

Awareness of sexual harassment and abuse has implications for how athletes understand what happens to them in sport, how they make judgements based upon personal ethics and perceptions of the sport roles, and how they understand right and wrong in the sporting context. Awareness, we believe, is a first step to athletes' preparedness to act, that is, of being able to resist if sexual discrimination or harassment and abuse occur. If and when athletes take on leadership roles in sport, they will be able to reproduce a quality sport environment for others which is free from such discriminations. Encouragingly, 80 percent of responding athletes consider sexual violence an issue.

Thus, of every 5 athletes, 2 think that harassment, assault and rape are all issues, 1 thinks that assault or sexual abuse is the issue, 1 thinks that sexual harassment alone is the issue and 1 thinks none of these are issues. Perhaps not surprisingly, female athletes are much more likely than males to think these are issues.[12]

Although it is heartening to see such a high awareness level amongst athletes, there is a difference between thinking something is an issue and actually being informed about it. It remains disturbing that 68 percent of the athletes received their information from sources outside of sport.[13] Only one-third of athletes heard about these issues specifically within the sporting context, and even then, mostly from other athletes. It appears that athletes may be somewhat informed about sexual harassment and abuse in sport but through education outside of sport. Within sport, athletes may be taking the lead in informing each other. If this is so, athletes may be protecting themselves and each other from sexual harassment and abuse while receiving little assistance from their sport organizations to do so. Although there is considerable discussion

Table 3: Awareness of the Issues
("Are these Issues in Sport?")

	Sexual Harassment?	Sexual Assault?	Sexual Abuse?	% of athletes who gave each Response Set
Response Sets	Yes	Yes	Yes	40%
	No	Yes	Yes	20%
	Yes	No	No	20%
	No	No	No	20%
% of athletes who responded, "Yes it is an issue in sports."	60%	60%	60%	

and program planning about sexual harassment and abuse in sport, it appears that the strategies being delivered across sport organizations are not reaching the athletes.

Sexual harassment/abuse are perceived differently by females and males, and the link between athletes' awareness and their belief in the need for action, particularly amongst female athletes, is a strong one. Females may understand that they are more at risk of sexual harassment and abuse than are males and that high performance sport, with its preponderance of males in positions of authority—including coaches, administrators and medical personnel—is a risky place to be. Female athletes, as some would say, are performing sport on a contested terrain, one previously occupied principally by males.

Feelings of Vulnerability, Safety and Fear
Athletes' responses to questions about feelings of vulnerability, safety and fear indicate to what extent there are negative conditions under which some athletes prepare for and compete at the high performance level.

Despite the relatively high awareness levels, only 13.9 percent of athletes feel personally vulnerable to harassment or abuse. Yet, the majority of athletes know abuses occur and can provide accounts of them. Many have personal experiences with such abuses. Yet, paradoxically, they do not seem to feel at risk. For example, when asked about feelings of vulnerability, only 37 of the 266 respondents gave a positive response (see Table 4).

Of those who did feel vulnerable, females (22.3 percent) are more

Table 4: Vulnerability in Sport by Gender

Gender of athletes who feel vulnerable (n = 37)			
	Female	Male	Total
Current Athletes	86.4%	13.6%	100% (p.< .002)
Retired Athletes	92.9%	7.1%	100%

Table 5: Vulnerability in Sport by Age

Percentage of all athletes who feel vulnerable			
	16–21 years	22–27 years	28+ years
Current Athletes	45.5%	40.9%	13.6%(p.<.04)
Retired Athletes	0.0 %	64.3%	35.7% (n.s.)

Table 6: Feelings of Safety

Feelings of safety in sport by gender			
	Very Safe	Less than Very Safe	Total
Female	80	66	146
Male	104	12	116
TOTAL	184	78	262

Athletes who are afraid, are afraid of different things:
1. rape/sexual assault (14.7 percent)
2. physical assault (4.9 percent)
3. sexual harassment (10.5 percent)
4. abuse of their children (7.1 percent)
5. other (3.4 percent)
6. multiple (5.6 percent)[15]

likely to feel vulnerable than males (3.4 percent, p.<000). Amongst current athletes who feel vulnerable, 86.4 percent are female (p.<002). Amongst retired athletes, the proportion of females increases to 92.9 percent. For those current and retired athletes who did not feel vulnerable, the gender breakdown is about 50/50. These figures show us that not only are female athletes more aware of the issues but proportionally more feel vulnerable than do their male counterparts even after they stop competing. Feelings of vulnerability decrease with the age of athletes (see Table 5).

However, since any feelings of vulnerability are counterproductive to a successful sport experience, it is distressing to note that 1 in 7 of all national-team athletes who responded to the survey feels vulnerable to some form of sexual violence.

How safe do athletes feel? One hundred and eighty-four athletes, 80 females and 104 males, or 69.5 percent, affirmed that they felt very safe in sport. This leaves slightly less than one-half of the females and one-tenth of the males, 29.3 percent of all athletes, feeling less than completely safe (see Table 6). [14] That any athlete feels less than very safe should be of considerable concern to researchers, coaches, administrators and others involved in the production and reproduction of sport.

Overall, more athletes are afraid (123) than feel vulnerable (78). Not all athletes who indicated they were afraid also indicated they felt vulnerable. And, when the results are shown with specific reference to gender, twice as many females as males are afraid in the sporting context. Not only are more female athletes afraid, they are afraid of different things than are males.

Table 7: Gender and Fear*

	Female	Male	Total
Rape/Sexual Assault	32 (39%)	7 (17%)	39 (31.7%)
Sexual Harassment	24 (29%)	4 (10%)	28 (22.7%)
Physical Harassment	5 (8%)	8 (20%)	13 (10.6%)
Multiple/Other	15 (18%)	9 (22%)	19 (15.4%)
Child Sexual Assault	6 (7%)	13 (32%)	24 (19.5%)
Total	82 (99%)	41 (101%)	123 (100%)

* Income shows a trend at p.< .009 (lower income is associated with fear) and Awareness of Issues is significant at p.< .001.

Table 7, with both the actual number of athletes who responded and percentages (percentaged across), illustrates that in the sporting context, female athletes are more afraid of rape/sexual assault and sexual harassment while male athletes are more afraid of physical assault, other/multiple behaviours and of sexual assault of their children (p.<000).

Our results on vulnerability, feelings of safety and fear show that fear of sexual violence in the sporting context is a reality for a significant number of athletes. While it is not unexpected to find women athletes more afraid of sexual harassment and abuse than male athletes, it was surprising that males indicated being more afraid of sexual assault on their children, proportionately the second largest category. This unexpected result has prompted many inquiries from the media about why such a finding exists. We interpret this in several ways. First, we believe this to be an indication of the degree to which males under-report their own sexual harassment and abuse experiences. They may have experienced or seen this type of abuse in the locker rooms, on team trips, or after their own training sessions. Second, males may have some insider knowledge about the degree to which children in sport fall prey to sexual predators. As the most successful of the athletes come through the system, they may be unwilling to report these occurrences for fear of risking their own sport careers. Another explanation may be that these athletes are aware of opportunities when they could have or did engage in sexual activity which could be seen as child sexual abuse. Clearly, we must ask male athletes why they fear child sexual abuse.

Athletes were subsequently asked if they could recall a specific event or a time in their sporting life that changed how safe they felt in sport. Roughly 20 percent of all respondents (61 athletes, 49 of them female) said "yes" and provided a description of the event or circumstance that made them feel less safe. Females describe roughly twice as many events which they say have influenced their fear than do males (p.<000). Given that the survey was about sexual violence, it is not surprising that the events reported almost exclusively involved sexual harassment and/or abuse.

Three themes emerge from the comments made by athletes who felt "less than very safe" in sport. First, they report a thriving sexist environment in some sport contexts which allows for sexually harassing attitudes and behaviours to flourish. Second, the perpetrator of the reported sexual harassment or abuse is often, though not always, a person in a position of power or authority over the athlete(s), usually a coach or someone providing medical support. Third, athletes may not be safe from other athletes. This points to the need to look not only at coach-athlete abuse, but at a wider spectrum of possible sources of abuse.

Thriving Sexist Environment
Athletes describe what appears to be a thriving sexist environment in high performance sport not unlike that of the chilly climate of the workplace (Joyce 1991; Lenskyj 1994). Athletes identified one or more of the following "poisoned environment" characteristics which made them feel less safe in sport:
1. verbal abuse which goes unchecked
2. sexual jokes
3. showing of pornographic videos, reviews and photos
4. sexual allusions about what athletes must do to make the team
5. tolerance of vulgar language
6. sexual comments about what athletes are wearing
7. tolerance of sexist and homophobic attitudes in coaches, particu-

larly those from other teams and/or other nations
8.   unwanted comments of a sexist and racist nature
9.   tolerance of sexual discrimination
10. tolerance of sexual harassment and abuse
These characteristics contribute to a sporting environment in which, as one athlete stated, "normalized" sexual comments and innuendo are a regular, condoned and tolerated part of sporting practice.

Some of this involved verbal abuse and some involved touching, as the following examples demonstrate:

> [My coach] sexually harassed the team by yelling, throwing (things) and spitting on the athletes. (015:23F)

> One of my teammates was nearly charged for sexual harassment because of his language towards other teammates. It had gotten to the point where we heard this language every day, we were desensitized to it. But charges opened our eyes to the serious wrongdoing. (118:24F)

These illustrate that some sport participants, including perpetrators of sexual harassment and abuse and those affected by it, are located within an environment where expressions of sexual predation can go somewhat unnoticed and without sanction from other athletes or coaches.

For some athletes, the link between sexism and sexual harassment is more direct:

> ... when a coach said to my team "Boy you look great in those sex suits, you all look like sex." Another coach that same week told a girl to "suck my dick" [while the athletes were changing positions during training]. He was both coaching and an athlete at the same time. (130:26F)

These comments allow us to look into the sexist part of the sport system, where sport participants, particularly female athletes, get bombarded with sexist commentary and desensitized to it through various everyday practices, and are still expected to provide a quality performance.

Some female athletes also feel a sense of vulnerability or helplessness in openly sexist circumstances, particularly when others do not step in to ameliorate the situation:

> I feel vulnerable ... when all the people in power positions

[coaches] are men and they don't stop verbal abuse by their colleagues and other men athletes on the team. (237:20F)

For some, the awareness of being sexually harassed and/or abused surfaces only after retirement from competition. Note that the following quote comes from a nineteen-year-old female athlete.

Now I am older and realize what sexual harassment is, I am aware that I was exposed to it as a younger athlete by my coach. At the time, I was fourteen and fifteen years old. (164:19F)

To use the analogy of a poisoned stream, if athletes are in a poisoned stream going with the current, removal from the stream (i.e., retirement) may be necessary before the athlete can see the pollutants in it (Canadian Council for Ethics and Sport 1995). As athletes become more experienced, they become more aware of the issues, the sexual behaviours or attitudes which are inappropriate. However, this same poisoned stream seems to flow right by some athletes, leaving them relatively unaffected. Overall, the lack of awareness of the effects of sexual harassment is worrisome because it shows a fundamental lack of concern for or perhaps awareness of the damage done to all sport participants when sexist language and actions go unattended and sanctioned.

Some athletes are aware of sexual harassment but responded that they simply did not feel at all vulnerable in the sporting environment. By way of illustration, one young male stated:

I never felt threatened or violated in any way but I am a male. (210:24M)

And two female athletes write:

I have personally never felt vulnerable or experienced anything that made me feel uncomfortable. (145:27F)

Not really, but all the boys in my sport are vulgar and make advances and allude to sex all the time. If they had the chance, I don't believe they would ever be able to do what they say they want to. (171:18F)

Importantly, only 2 of the 12 males who indicated that events had occurred which made them feel less safe in sport gave any indication that sexism, or the tolerance of it, affected their own sporting experience. It may be that men, even men who have been sexually abused, do not interpret their "less than safe" experiences in sport as vulnerability. They may have a completely different attitude to what is unsafe versus what is vulnerability. Maleness itself, apparently, affords some protection against feelings of vulnerability in a chilly sport climate.

The expressions of infallibility among female athletes may be indicative of high achievers who feel somewhat protected by their skill base and reputation in sport. This lack of awareness of the impact of the chilly climate on themselves or other athletes ensures that such athletes remain uninterested bystanders even if they do see or hear about sexual abuse experiences. The need for education of athletes, from very young ages, has never been more clear. Education about their right to enjoy sport free from sexual harassment and abuse and about sharpening their skills in recognizing such discriminations are important steps towards eradicating these from sport.

Perpetrators in Positions of Authority

Of those athletes who feel less than very safe in sport, many wrote about specific instances involving authority figures which made them think differently about their safety. This is instructive because perhaps for the first time, we have a window through which to see the treatment of some of our most high profile athletes at the hands of their coaches and other persons in positions of authority. The athletes provide for us, the readers, some critical information about grooming and abuse of power by those who are trusted and upon whom the athletes are somewhat dependent.

We have divided this section into subsections dealing with the particular groups of persons reported to be involved in the incidents which upset the athletes enough to make them feel vulnerable in sport. Although coaches, as a group, are the most frequently implicated, athletes also report occasions involving physiotherapists, medical doctors and sport administrators. Note that all accounts involve elements of unwanted sexual attention that the athletes have witnessed or experienced. These accounts are provided specifically in response to athletes' experiencing an increased sense of vulnerability.

Coaches

Coaches are in a position of authority over athletes in their charge. That authority may be temporary, in place for a single training session or single international competition, or may be relatively permanent and based on several years of interaction. Coaches have a primary responsibility to athletes, that of facilitating the athletes' needs as they proceed along their sport career paths. Generally, coaches are accorded considerable authority and freedom to do the job as they see fit. As a group, they have a great deal of integrity and are well-trained professionals capable of handling considerable responsibility. They work with very talented and hardworking athletes to facilitate the development of athletic successes, and to do this, they are in frequent contact with these individuals. The contact they have may take many forms, from the physical, psychological and social to the educational, financial and emotional. Most coaches are in daily contact with the high performance athletes. At the elite level coaches are almost always male and often there is a considerable age difference between the coaches and the athletes in their care, particularly in sports where the athletes peak at a young age.

Being a good coach means coaching responsibly, that is, with the best interests of the athletes at the centre of the work. So too, most coaches are powerful role models. They recognize the power of the coaching position and with that, their ability to affect the development of athletes' values and capabilities. The successful coach-athlete relationship is a mutually respectful one where, for example, all the athletes feel "equally worthy as persons."[16] Coaches are responsible for establishing the "respectful workplace," a "respectful sport place," which includes the promotion of the dignity and rights of all participants, of the profession of coaching, and of the "mutual support among fellow coaches, officials and athletes and their family members" (Tomlinson and Strachan 1996:93).

However, from the frequency of athletes' reports, we see that coaches are the principle abusers of athletes in sport. Remembering that respondents are relating events which made them feel more vulnerable, the following accounts indicate that coaches are involved in sexual harassment and assault of athletes and others.

Coaches are reported to have sexually harassed athletes in a variety of ways. Here are two examples, one account from a female athlete, the other from a male athlete.

> Athletes on my team were complaining because the male coaches wanted to sleep with them—one lost her place on the team because of it. She complained. (200:36F)

> A male coach harassed a sixteen-year-old girl on team trips and during regular training. The coach continually isolated himself with her on road trips in so-called player meetings and hinted towards sexual encounters. He was then extra hard on her during practices, criticizing her so it looked like she wasn't getting special attention. (137:25M)

In the first example, the compromise offered by the coach to the athlete had no place in sport. In the second, the coach made one athlete a target of his sexual efforts and destroyed that athlete's sense of security, fairness and comfort in sport. The coach's efforts to compensate for his lack of judgement further penalized the harassed athlete by unfair treatment during practice, in front of her teammates. Her efforts to achieve athletic success were truly compromised. Further, the coach destroyed team cohesion by selecting one athlete for special negative treatment. Athletes must always be assured that their place on a team is because of their abilities, not because the coach wants to establish or maintain sexual access to them or others on the team.

There are other ways in which coaches express sexual interest in athletes, and such behaviour may cause athletes to change coaches, change teams or even withdraw from elite level sport (074:30F). The following are just two of many examples of coaches who tried to sexually "hit on" athletes:

> An assistant coach asking if there was any chance of he and I getting together as a couple. (225:31F)

> A provincial coach and national-team committee member making sexual advances on me. (234:24F)

When coaches are in a position of trust over athletes, a certain relationship of dependence exists. Coaches who think of athletes as potential sexual partners are betraying or breaching this trust (Brackenridge 1997b), and it is difficult for athletes to refuse, particularly if the coach (or the national-team committee member) has a significant influence over the career opportunities for the athletes. If this is a choice being presented to athletes, it is a choice of one.

Equally disturbing is that some coaches choose very young athletes as their sexual targets. In the following case, the athlete even expressed some sense of responsibility for having been at risk, a not unusual feeling for those who are harassed or abused. The athlete feels responsible despite knowing that the coach involved was in a position of power over her and "should have known better."

> At age sixteen, at a sport event, without adequate supervision, I put myself in a vulnerable position which I regret [with a coach]. However, it possibly could have been prevented if adult supervision was demanded at youth events. (123:25F)

The difference between a good coach and one who "crosses the line" lies in the ability of the coach to set appropriate personal and professional boundaries for her/himself and for the team. Improved discipline and supervision are needed for both coaches and athletes to ensure that no one gets involved in compromising positions.

The last example here is of a coach who used his position of power over the team to set an inappropriate sexist and sexual standard of behaviour for the athletes.

> A coach was always telling the young athletes to go to his place and he would put on pornographic videos and show pornographic photos. I was made to go one time to see that. I was furious. The others thought it was funny. (031:36F)

The athletes were encouraged as part of the team-building exercise, to participate in the viewing of pornographic videos. It is problematic to assume that athletes have freedom of choice about whether to attend. If the coach sets this "for the team," then to remain part of the team, athletes will feel compelled to participate even if they know it is wrong. The athlete in the above example chose not to return. As a result, she felt a certain ostracism from the team but was more disturbed that the other young athletes remained uncritical of the activities of the coach. While the line between pornography and sexual violence is a complicated one, research (Kelly et. al. 1995) indicates an active role of pornography in some sexual-abuse, particularly child-sexual-abuse, cases. The coach in the above example is obviously providing not only poor role modelling but support for outright sexism in his coaching practice, and athletes and their parents should not tolerate such inappropriate behaviour.

Athletes also report that their coaches had sexually assaulted others:

> My sister was abused by our coach although I didn't realize it until she retired. (255:37F)

> I found out my ex-coach had molested a younger student of his. He was jailed for it. (232:19F)

Both of these athletes are in the uncomfortable position of finding out about sexual abuse after the fact. If an effective criminal screening process had been in place, the coach in the second example would never have been allowed to coach. The first example illustrates the athletes' sense of insecurity when they have been abused but feel they can't talk about it, except perhaps with their closest friends in sport. Other athletes could unknowingly have been at personal risk from these coaches. In the next examples, athletes report that some coaches had ongoing sexual relationships with team members. This abuse continues apparently even if it is well known amongst the team members.

> One coach had multiple relationships with the women athletes. The coach dated two thirds of the women's team over two years. (212:26M)

> Yes, in artistic gymnastics. Our coach, a man who was twenty-four years old, marginal, manipulative and influential, fell in love with one of my friends, a gymnast also. We were twelve, thirteen, fourteen years old. I witnessed some of the sexual touching. (033:22F)

The activities of the coach who had multiple relationships with his team and of the coach who "fell in love" with the twelve- to fourteen-year-old gymnast are known to the other athletes, though no formal complaints followed these situations. In the first example, even if the athletes are "of age,"[17] sexual abuse exists because the coach is in a position of authority and trust with those athletes. He took advantage of the coach-athlete relationship to gain sexual access. When twelve- to fourteen-year-old girls are involved, a case for child sexual abuse might be indicated. When coaches use their professional relationship for sexual purposes, they are sexually exploiting athletes in their care.

The final quote indicates perhaps a more stereotypical form of sexual assault.

> I remember seeing my coach touch a fellow athlete in a private area. I saw her shock and terror. I knew then something should be done. (244:28M)

The athlete who saw this didn't know what needed to be done but did know that good coaches do not touch athletes in a sexual manner. One of the possible issues here is that because much of the sexual violence is "behind closed doors" (i.e., that it is "known" but not generally "seen" by the athletes), when athletes actually witness sexual assault, they must be ready to act. Often, the person who is assaulted feels powerless to act without support or witnesses. Another issue is the very unsettling realization that one is being or has been coached by someone who has sexual motives, even if the athlete is not her/himself the target. Certainly there are more victims of sexual violence than just those who are primarily victimized.

All of the examples so far paint a disturbing picture of the kinds of sexual harassment and abuse perpetrated by coaches. The coach-athlete relationship is an important one and it should stand up to public scrutiny. While it is often necessary for coaches to know very personal information about athletes in order to provide training and competition experiences which fit well with the athletes' goals and talents, they do not, and should not, have any sexual interest in athletes they coach.

Figure 3: Sexual Abuse in Relationships of Trust Authority and Relationships of Dependency: Some Examples

• teacher/student relationship (Dubé 1997, A1.; R. v Horne [1987] NWTR 168 (SC); Buchanon 1997, B1) • scout master/scout ("Former Boy Scout" A-11.; R v. Robertson (1979), 46 CCC (2d) 573; 10 CR (3d) S-46 (Ont.CA))
• doctor/patient (O'Hanlon 1997)
• big brother/young person in his charge (R. v. Vandermay (1984), 56 AR 239 (CA))
• football coach/young player • coach/young male hockey players • coach/young female gymnasts (R. v. Cramp, [1987] BCJ no. 2705 (Co. Ct.); Board 1997, C6; Rinehart 1996)
• priest/altar boy or • member of senior religious order/young male and female school residents (R. v. Kelly (1988), 68 Nfld. & PEIR 236 (Nfld, CA); "Accusations d'agressions physiques et sexuelles," E-7)
• workers in reform school/young male residents ("At Three Reform Schools")
• First Nations Band administrator/young boy band member (R. v. Roach (1987), 3 YR 57 (SC))
• adult employer/young person employee (R. v. G. (T.F.) (1992), 11 CR (4th) 221; 55 OAC 355 (CA)) • volunteer childcare worker/very young children in his care (Haysom 1997)

Nor should coaches use their positions of power to gain sexual access to people in their charge. Further, coaches have an additional responsibility for ensuring that athletes, who are sometimes very young, are properly supervised and do not come to harm. If coaches abuse that trust to gain sexual access to the athletes, it is not unlike other breaches of trust or authority in cases where a relationship of dependency exists (See Figure 3).

Physiotherapists, Medical Doctors and Sport Administrators
Physiotherapy is a task for well-trained professionals. They have codes of ethics which guide what is appropriate treatment and behaviour within a professional/client relationship. We have indications here that athletes' safety has been compromised by instances of sexual harassment and abuse where the perpetrators are therapists/physiotherapists or, in one case, that of a coach taking on the responsibility of a physiotherapist.

> In competition, one night, I was massaged by the athletic therapist for the first time and he rubbed his penis on my hip. (041:31M)

In this example, the therapist "crossed the line," taking out his penis and rubbing it against the hip of the athlete The athlete was having his first, and we hope last, massage by this athletic therapist. Athletes should also be warned about coaches who actually go beyond the coaching role. This example is an important signal to athletes. They should be able to say "this is inappropriate behaviour," whether it occurs with an athletic therapist, a physiotherapist or another person performing these functions.

The subsequent examples demonstrate how sexual harassment and abuse can enter into some of the therapist/athlete relationships in sport.

> I felt uncomfortable by the friendly nature of one therapist. He was later charged [for sexual harassment] by someone else and found not guilty. (050:26F)

> Allegations were made by a fellow teammate about a team physiotherapist involving sexual touching. (238:28F)

> I was sexually harassed and assaulted. There was nowhere to go for help. I eventually filed a complaint. He [the therapist] was found not guilty for lack of evidence. I could have used some help. Both mentally and financially. Now in process of appeal. (049:23F)

In these examples, two of the three physiotherapists are male, one is not identified by sex. The athletes reporting these are all female. Complaints or charges were made by athletes, though in the first case, not immediately. Interestingly, it is there that an athlete's intuition warns her of potential danger. Jointly these suggest that physiotherapists need to be carefully screened and their access to athletes needs to be much more carefully monitored.

The final example raises critical questions about required treatments:

> Ladies have groin pulls and need preventative wraps. It is common to drop your shorts and have the therapist wrap over your bike shorts or panties. This therapist would go under the underwear "in case you have to go to the bathroom." (050:26F)

Is this the usual practice for physiotherapists? If so, they should give better reasons; ones the athletes can believe. If not, this would surely be a cause for a complaint by an athlete offended at such treatment. In all examples involving physiotherapists, the athletes were "treated" in ways that made them feel uncomfortable. More insidious is the way in which professionals can use their positions to convince athletes that what they are experiencing is "just accepted practice," thus ensuring that athletes won't believe they can complain.

Like physiotherapists, medical doctors are named in sexual harassment and abuse situations with athletes, though not with near the frequency of coaches or physiotherapists. See for example:

> When one of the team doctors was hitting on one of the athletes. (215:20F)

> It involved drug testing after a race. A male doctor was sent with the woman into the bathroom to watch her urinate, not a woman. This would be totally unacceptable to me. (067:21F)

Once more, these illustrate the need for clear boundaries, this time between the doctor and the athlete/patient, something about which the Canadian College of Physicians and Surgeons has been very proactive.[18] The last example however raises an interesting point about what rights athletes have if they are in a different nation during competition and are being treated or subjected to particular tests by medical people not from their own country. The drug-testing program is already a difficult experience for athletes without their having to face additional unsettling events such as the one above. The accepted practice for drug testing is consistent nationally and internationally (Parker 1997). The observer may or may not be a medical person but must be of the same sex as the athlete providing the sample. The Canadian Council for Ethics in Sport (CCES) recommends that if Canadian athletes are faced with such a situation, they should question the process even before providing the required sample and/or complete the supplementary report forms which are available for athletes to make any complaints or comments (Parker, 1997; Canadian Council for Drug-free Sport, n.d.).

There is only one reported instance of an athlete feeling more vulnerable because of the actions of a sport administrator.

> Our ED [Executive Director] was the manager on the trip. He was drunk and jumped on one of our athletes. We [the members] put forward a rule that a parent has to be present on all out-of-town competitions when juniors are involved. We should have fired this person, but he got a warning and a one-year probation. (133:30F)

Team travel is not a licence for inappropriate behaviour, nor, in this case, child sexual assault. This needs no further comment about the breaching of trust, the inappropriateness of the actions, the role of alcohol abuse in instances of sexual violence or the effect such behaviour has on athletes, particularly junior athletes. What is encouraging here is the action taken by the athletes to better ensure their safety.

All of the above examples involve professionals—coaches, physiotherapists, physicians and, in one case, a sport administrator—acting inappropriately towards athletes. In combination, the elements of exploitation, breach of trust, criminal behaviour, poor decision-making and sexual predation can be found in the athletes' accounts of what has made them feel more vulnerable in sport. The current standard of "they are professionals. Let them do their job" seems hugely inappropriate in the face of these abuses.

From the respondents' reports, we have calculated that complaints or charges were laid in 8.3 percent of these situations with coaches and in 55.6 percent of situations involving physiotherapists or physicians. It may be that athletes find it easier to make a complaint against a professional physiotherapist than they do against their personal coach. Perhaps athletes understand the accepted practices of physiotherapy more clearly than the appropriate limits to coaching. It may also be that because the chilly climate is somewhat normalized in sport, athletes only "see" sexual harassment and abuse as such if it occurs outside the immediate context of sport.

Strangers or Other Athletes

Two other groups of people are implicated in events which make athletes feel more vulnerable in sport. Although these people may not have positions of authority over the athletes, both total strangers and, perhaps surprisingly, other athletes are portrayed as being part of the sexual violence problem.

Many of these events related by the athletes occurred when they were on team trips. For example, as one athlete reports, she and a couple of other athletes were harassed after competition outside of Canada.

> When I was at a train station in [a foreign country] and it was me with two other women [athletes] and these men crowded around us. (163:20F)

Partly, athletes are more vulnerable when they are travelling because they are distant from known standards of behaviour and key social supports. It is also disturbing that young Canadian athletes may find themselves unprotected from groups of strangers when abroad. This illustrates yet again the need for improved planning and supervision of athletes while travelling.

Successful athletes describe harassment problems arising from a "fishbowl" existence, where people seem to regard the athletes as public property. For example, one very young female athlete wrote that she was harassed by strangers after becoming the subject of sports reporting on her athletic achievements and home life.

> After some competitions were reported in the newspaper, I received harassing phone calls from male callers. (001:14F)

Such experiences leave athletes feeling vulnerable to public scrutiny while at the same time with little control over what is reported about them. Some athletes have even experienced being stalked by strangers simply because they were well known. There is a need for sensitive media coverage that actually reduces rather than increases the risks athletes face as they become increasingly famous.

Several athletes report actually being attacked by strangers. This example is from a female athlete pursued by a male stranger during a training run:

> In a park, instead of taking the path, I decided to run on the roads parallel to the path because it was dusk and the sun was going down. An individual, a male, began to follow me by cutting through the woods to cross the path ahead of me. I was

able to save myself by finding, about a half kilometre ahead, a police car. I told my story to the officer. (183:35F)

The physical and social isolation of this athlete during her training is not the cause of the harassment she experienced. Rather, it is indicative of the risky situations that athletes may find themselves in while they are focused on their training.

Physical and/or social isolation of the athletes is apparent in virtually all harassing situations. With strangers, first a group of female athletes was isolated by a group of men at a train station, second, an athlete was selected for sexual attention because of her public visibility and third, what should have been a pleasant end of the day "steady state run" was turned into a fearful experience. Further, although children can be abused by strangers, most are abused by adults they know and trust (North Kesteven District Council et al 1997). Athletes, whether children or adults, may be more at risk from strangers because of the public nature of sport training and competition, their media visibility and their exposure to strangers during travel on team trips.

Athletes are not always safe with other athletes. A number of athletes report incidences with other athletes, some on their own teams, others not, who made them feel more vulnerable in the sporting context. In the first four situations highlighted here, athletes report receiving unwanted sexual attention from their peers. The first two involve sexual touching without consent.

Another athlete my age, when we were both younger, touched my breasts without my consent. (036:25F)

I am in a contact sport and sometimes I've been touched and asked myself if my opponent did it on purpose or if it was by accident, like a hand between legs or a hand on breast. (103:29F)

Athletes do not have the right to any more sexual access to each other than do peers in non-sport contexts. The first example is a case of sexual touching without consent. So is the second, although it arises during the performance of the sport. Some coaches have raised the point that touching is required in sport, that is, that the athlete must be touched in certain ways to perform the sport or to learn the sport. While touching may be necessary, touching which makes the athlete uncomfortable or is of a sexual nature has no place in the learning or performance of sport. As is true in all cases of sexual harassment, that the touching is unwanted and makes a person feel uncomfortable is more important than the intent, however innocent, of the person doing the touching.

Are athletes sexually available to each other? Since sport is also a social experience, athletes may participate in team gatherings such as parties, fundraisers or hazings. The majority of sexual contact amongst athletes is socially acceptable—between peers, consensual and appropriate. However, there are cases where athletes abuse other athletes, using the sport milieu for the inappropriate expression of sexual motives. See, for example, the following:

> During a party, he became drunk and disagreeable. He made all sorts of unpleasant sexual advances. (192:20F)

This account illustrates the link between alcohol use and sexual aggression. We are aware of several other cases where athletes have reported that coaches and others above the legal drinking age purchased alcohol for the use of under-age athletes. Parents cannot necessarily assume that their children are being carefully supervised. The vulnerability of athletes, particularly under-age athletes, is increased when the use of alcohol is combined with team events. Supervision of such events will only go part of the way to ensuring that athletes are safe. Athletes who are educated about harassment and alcohol abuse should be able to fully and safely enjoy team functions.

The next two accounts illustrate some of the forms sexual abuse can take. In the first, a male athlete pressured a female athlete to have sex. She got scared and managed to end the threat by withdrawing.

> Yes. A friend I was with wanted to sleep with me. I didn't. He said "I don't want to hurt you." I got out of there like lightning. [Note: she explains that she also does martial arts so feels like she has the necessary physical and mental skills to deal with such a situation]. (119:29F)

The second athlete was sexually assaulted by an athlete she trusted.

> [I was] raped by a member of the local club team who was also my boyfriend. (256:36F)

The fact of knowing other athletes is little protection against sexual assault. As with sexual assault in other situations, sexual assault in sport often involves perpetrators who are known, even very well known, and trusted by the victims. This suggests that not only is better supervision important, but sport organizations should actively discourage sexually predatory behaviour when it first occurs amongst athletes.

The final two accounts return to the situation of the particular vulnerabilities of athletes during international travel, a time when they are removed from their social and emotional supports. They may be faced with large numbers of people from different teams, both males and females, with unfamiliar ways of behaving and, after competitions, with a "big party" atmosphere. At international games, where athletes are (usually) outside the home country and housed in athletes' villages, large gatherings of male athletes, particularly those in teams, are unsettling for female athletes.

> After attending a multi-sport competition we had stricter rules and regulations because the facility and accommodations were a mix of men and women of all ages. (051:15F)

One of the problems reported by female athletes was that they were confronted individually or in pairs by groups of male athletes from other cultures. Also, the "twenty-four-hour services" program, particularly at Olympic Games, meant that supervision of all athletes at all times was almost impossible. Greater risk is created if those responsible for supervising an international team take a "holiday-approach" to the experience once the actual competition is over. Together, these problems create an environment where even the strongest athlete may feel less than safe.

In sum, within the context of this survey, athletes feel their safety is compromised because they have heard, seen or experienced sexual violence. However, very little of what is heard, seen or experienced is ever reported publicly or through a complaint process. Moreover, since much of our reported information falls into the "hearsay" category, we must conclude that not only do athletes feel vulnerable because they have experienced harassment or abuse themselves, but also because these things occur or are rumoured to occur to others. We can also surmise that when sexual harassment and abuse occur, there is a dome of silence over virtually all athletes, coaches and others who "know." No one "talks" about what is occurring—either because it is regarded as "normal behaviour," because they are unsure of what to say to whom or because they fear of the consequences of speaking out. Additionally, the poisoned environment ensures that there is some desensitization of athletes, and others, to the impact of sexual violence. This in turn means that many athletes and coaches appear to be socialized into remaining "disinterested bystanders" even when they do see or hear of sexual violence problems.

We conclude that a significant number of athletes feel vulnerable, think they are less than very safe in sporting situations and are particularly concerned for the safety of children. If 30 percent of athletes do not feel safe in the sport context and if proportionally more of these are female athletes, then Canadian sport and its leaders face a major challenge in making sport safe for all athletes and particularly for female athletes. Improved media coverage, supervision and chaperoning, education on the effects of sexism, alcohol abuse and sexual violence, plus enhanced scrutiny of behaviour amongst particularly coaches and medical professionals have all been identified as ways to improve sport. Every sport participant deserves a quality, safe experience. We believe, without a doubt, that athletes' feelings of lack of safety are a major cause for alarm.

What Athletes Have Seen or Heard about Sexual Harassment

Rumour and innuendo about sexual harassment and abuse seem to be alive and well in sport. Although this informal "rumour mill" may warn athletes of potentially dangerous situations, it does little to curtail the problems at the root of the rumours. In one particularly startling example, the paradoxical position of sport organizations is revealed. In a national broadcast (CBC 1993), one national sport organization representative encouraged athletes to pay attention to the rumour mill to "protect themselves." This warning stemmed from a sexual harassment complaint, the results of which were confidential and thus freed the organization from responsibility for the "guilty coach." Later, on the same program, another official from the organization indicated it could not rely on rumours when it came to hiring coaches. Although the positions taken by both representatives are understandable, neither is athlete-centred, nor would either protect athletes from situations involving potential harm. Clearly, rumours are not to be trusted, yet associations need to follow up rumours in a serious manner. If further action is required, the organization should ensure all its members are safe and are treated respectfully and fairly in any complaint process.

We asked athletes to describe what they had been witness to or what they had heard about sexual violence to see if we could somehow grasp the extent and content of the rumour mill. This section relates the athletes' reports about the rumour mill. We found that one out of every two athletes (52 percent) is directly aware of particular rumours or has witnessed specific events in the sporting environment which touch upon sexual harassment or abuse.

Athletes were asked to recount only the most upsetting incident, and 61 of these 140 incidents occurred on team trips (see Figure 4).

About twice as many female athletes see or hear about sexual harassment and abuse situations as do males. Also, many respondents described incidents which involved behaviours in more than one place or which victimized several athletes. This shows that when sexual harass-

Figure 4: Where does Harassment and Abuse Occur?

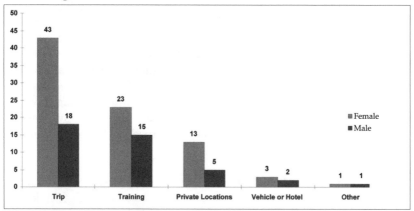

Table 8: Sex of Reporting Athlete
by Persons Implicated in Rumours and Events Witnessed

	Female Athlete	Male Athlete	Total
Coach	48	20	69*
Athlete	9	3	12
Medical/			
Physiotherapist	5	3	8
Stranger	5	0	5
Administrator	2	0	2
* One individual did not indicate sex			

ment/abuse in sport occurs, it appears as an ongoing, repeated activity which happens in a number of places, rather than an isolated occurrence restricted to a single and predictable site.

When we asked athletes to tell us what they had seen or heard about the experiences of other athletes, many accounts emerged. Some athletes provided their personal accounts. Others told us of situations they knew about. In some cases, we suspected that the athletes might have been writing about themselves even though they were using the voice of a third person.

First, we asked if athletes were aware of situations in which sexual harassment and/or abuse had occurred and, if so, to describe the situation which was most upsetting, including information on where the situation occurred. Of the 96 who responded, 69 wrote about situations involving coaches, 12 about other athletes, 5 about medical doctors, 3 about physiotherapists, 5 about strangers, and 1 each about a national-team committee member and a manager of a sport site. Coaches top the list as those implicated in rumours or incidents which athletes have witnessed. Table 8 illustrates who is hearing and seeing what.

In total, more than one-third of all athletes described at least one incident that happened to others in their own or another sport. Of these, 72 percent of the reports come from female athletes and 27 percent from male athletes. Since 55 percent of our respondents were female, female athletes are proportionally more aware of specific incidences than are male athletes. Remember that these reports are different than those reported in the previous section on safety and are also different from the section that follows on what the athletes themselves have experienced.

Coaches
Overall, 72 percent of the reports are of sexual harassment and abuse by coaches. Almost all of these involve male coaches with female athletes (81 percent). The sexual harassment and abuse by coaches is reported to occur during regular training (34 percent), on team trips (25 percent), in hotels/motels or billets (14 percent), in private locations such as the coach's home or office (13 percent), in vehicles (6 percent), in public locations (3 percent) and other sites (5 percent).

Male Coaches to Female Athletes: Groomed Sexual Encounters
By far, the largest category of response cites male coaches initially establishing close, "loving" relationships with female athletes, and then sexually harassing and/or abusing them. It appears that coaches groom athletes for sexual encounters and as sexual partners. These rumoured sexual encounters take many forms, and many involve coaches pursuing relationships with much younger athletes. In the first example, the coach used the pretext of a "private coaching session" to persuade an athlete to come to his hotel room and then applied pressure to gain sexual access:

> A coach who was fifteen years older than me hit on me! It was on team trips and during regular training. I was eighteen and it was my first time on Senior National Team. I went to his room because we were all to have individual meetings and it was my turn, anyway—instead of talking about how I did, he told me I was beautiful, that he had a hard time resisting me. Then he sat beside me on the bed and we continued to talk. Then he started kissing me. I did not ask him not to. I was afraid and I couldn't believe my coach liked me!?? Next time we got together (two months later), he snuck into my room and started necking with me. I told him we shouldn't but he said it was "okay"! Later on that week he tried to have sex with me. (002:F)

Here we see the raw power a coach can use to coax an athlete into sex by grooming her over several sessions. This puts her at a severe disadvantage, and, although she is flattered by the coach's attentions, she knows the whole scenario is wrong. The athlete clearly feels that her relationship with the coach has ceased to be professional.

Three other examples illustrate some of the characteristics of the abusive coach-athlete relationship.

> A much older coach [thiry-five] became sexually involved with a young [seventeen-year-old] athlete and manipulated her into acts of defiance against her former coach, sport governing body and eventually her family. She left home to live with him in a foreign country and had not contacted them in over a year. I don't know if this qualifies as abuse or harassment but I think it's still an exploitation of power and probably significant. (246:21F)

> A thirty-year-old coach I know was sleeping with a fifteen-year-old [team] member while on road trips. She was his girlfriend at the time. (130:26F)

> Older male coaches going after young girls, fourteen-year-old girls that they have known since they were kids. These harassments occurred during regular training, sometimes at his place or at the hotel when we were travelling. I also know another coach who pursued a fourteen-year-old girl. He was thirty, very charming. They had a relationship and then he left her. Needless to say, she had many problems. It became a pattern, there were other girls all under seventeen years. Isn't this statutory rape? (184:21F)

The athletes reporting these events seem unsure about whether or not they constitute breaches of trust and/or sexual assault. Even though the coaches and, possibly the athletes, in these cases might suggest the sexual encounters are consensual, consent cannot be given when one person is in a position of authority over another. Second, even if coaches had not actually been in a position of authority over the younger athletes, the age difference between the athletes and the coaches is extreme, making an egalitarian relationship difficult to imagine. We must also consider the age of the athletes. In two of the three examples just provided, the sexual abuse is also child sexual abuse.

The following account illustrates the horrendous effects of sexual assault involving the sexual grooming of an athlete:

One of my teammates had slept with the coach (forty-three years old when it started) since she was thirteen. She felt awful because she couldn't say anything to anybody. The sexual abuse happened on team trips, in his trailer, in his vehicle, in the hotel and in many other places. The coach said how special she was, and he took her on as his special project. He coached her as his special project, so special that he slept with her until she was eighteen. He completely isolated her from the rest of us. After the Olympic Games, she quit sport because, as she said, he was the only coach in her city and she had to get away from him. She has since had two failed marriages. She never reported him, BUT STILL COULD! (200:36F)

Here, a pedophile/coach successfully groomed a high performance athlete and sexually exploited her for five years. This occurred "under the noses" of the National Sport Association, the Canadian Olympic Association, her teammates and her parents. One can only imagine how this young athlete must have felt at the pinnacle of athletic achievement, the Olympic Games, or how carrying this "guilty knowledge" must have affected the athlete who reports this account.

The next example illustrates just how thin is the veneer of a "relationship" over sexual harassment and abuse.

The situation was harassment and it was by a friend in a position of power, my coach. The use of the position was not even recognized by him. The abuse happened in his home. It's difficult to describe. It was more of an ongoing situation where coach/athlete/friend was beginning to get confusing—when were you just a friend or athlete or coach? When you work closely with someone for so long, it [the relationship] gets taken for granted and people feel they can say or do anything they want. (120:28F)

Even though some athletes are aware of the way coaches can misuse authority (074:30F) and aware of the favouritism coaches may use to obtain sexual contact with athletes, they seem somewhat uncritical of coaches who "date" athletes unless the athletes are particularly young. That sexual assaults are generally unreported has allowed two things to occur: The coaches continue to abuse the athletes with impunity. The damage done to the athletes and to their sport careers remains profound.

Male Coaches to Female Athletes: Sexual Encounters without Grooming
There are numerous accounts of coaches "crossing the line" and sexually assaulting female athletes without the pretence of a relationship. In many cases, the coaches simply gain access to particular athletes on team trips or during regular training. Sometimes the sexual assaults are single encounters. Other times, there are systematic assaults over a period of time on a single athlete or on several athletes. Some coaches are "obsessed by the body size and type of athletes," while others promise the athletes "a relationship." See the following examples:

> A coach who used his authority to take advantage of students, during regular training and also at his home. A long-time coach with a close and trusting relationship with student began inviting her to his home for "extra" training-related sessions. He subtly began to sexually harass/molest her in such a way that she was afraid to speak up about the issue for a long period of time. (064:19F)

> When the coach sleeps around with his athletes in an ongoing [way], [the coach is], in my mind, preying on them from a position of trust, despite the fact that both the coach and the athletes would likely claim that the sex was consensual. (157:28F)

These and several other reports identified coaches, all male, who were rumoured to be sexually active with their female athletes on team trips, during regular training and in hotels.[19] Others report that they were taken advantage of by coaches because they found themselves in vulnerable positions such as being transported home from a practice,[20] getting into compromising situations in the celebrations which often occur after major competitions, while in the coach's house,[21] or simply because they were "rookies" or students and not yet knowledgeable in the ways to keep themselves safe.[22]

Despite the fact that consensual sex between a coach and his athletes is an impossibility because of the position of authority he has over those athletes, coaches appear to engage in such activities virtually without penalty. In one instance a coach was even reported to be sexually active with the majority of his team.

Male Coaches to Female Athletes: Sexual Harassment
The athletes are aware of various forms of sexual harassment. Some describe "flirtations by coach to athletes ... saying unnecessary things suggestively to athletes"—the velvet glove approach. Others describe the environment in which female athletes must practise, an environ-

ment poisoned by sexism which is generated by the coaches. Some coaches feel it is their place to touch the athletes in ways that are not essential to the performance of the sport (e.g., body-fat testing in an intimate setting). Coaches also comment on female athletes' breast sizes or body shapes, try to "pick up" players because they are single, dress inappropriately (e.g., "where we saw the crack of his butt") in front of the athletes or are condescending specifically to female athletes.

At other times, the sexual harassment is more overt, where it is accompanied again, by other forms of harassment:

> The coach was harassing one of my fellow athletes in a number of situations ... making harsh, degrading comments towards women in general and those on the team. I know from testimony of an assaulted athlete that he harassed her. (046:21M)

> The sexist coach of women's team was ... too "touchy" during regular training. He was also verbally abusive, sexist and he liked to get too close to the women during "private" coaching, (095:21M)

Sexual harassment in sport can survive in a very public arena, for example, during team practices. The first account is reminiscent of the kind of abusive language used by some coaches on female athletes at the Atlanta Olympic Games. Those televised occurrences drew public comment about the inappropriateness of such a "style of coaching" and of the abusive language coaches "hurled at athletes." The second account is a yet another warning to athletes about the dangers of "private coaching" sessions.

What did the athletes do about the sexual harassment and abuse? Mostly, they put up with it, complaining within their group but not talking about it publicly. Even when the public was witness to the abuse, nothing was said. This dome of silence allows for intolerable treatment of athletes to go on for as long as the coach wishes. One athlete reports watching as one of her teammates "lost her position on a team because of gender differences and turned down advances" (101:20F). Another had been taken into the confidence of a teammate about sexual abuse but could not describe the situation because "I would rather not. I promised the individual that I'd never say anything" (117:22F). The silence is deafening in both cases.

The final example in this section is somewhat more hopeful. An athlete, who also coaches, is aware of her responsibility to intervene:

I was coaching a recreational class with a male coach who was known to be a slime. I had been teaching awhile when a female student contacted me informing me that the male coach was being very aggressive, phoning, showing up at her work, etc. I approached him. He denied it and made up an excuse. I didn't believe him. This happened during regular training, in private locations, at his home and at work. Another situation was where a male coach was playing sugar daddy to one of the under-fifteen-year-old girls, buying things for her on trips, encouraging her that hugging him was good, that it was okay for him to massage her, to hold her hand. I spoke to her mother, but the mother wasn't concerned even though others besides myself didn't like what we saw, including some of the girl's peers. (204:34F)

The attention this coach-athlete gave to each situation is encouraging; making perpetrators aware that they were being watched is an excellent strategy. Also, it illustrates that a coach can take responsibility for speaking out when the safety of athletes is being compromised by coaching colleagues.

Male Coaches to Female Athletes: Poisoned Environment
As we have stated earlier, coaches should be competent, respectful and ethical. In other words, they should be well prepared, treat athletes (clients) with respect, and think and act in morally responsible ways. As Tomlinson and Strachan say, "coaches continually use their power through the choices they make about how they relate to athletes and others in sport" (1996:3). When these choices are informed by sexual motives, a poisoned environment, in which sexual harassment and abuse occur, is created and maintained. In the following, the coach is described as actively cultivating sexist attitudes through the use of pornographic videos, magazines and sex-talk.

The coach who continued to show pornographic videos to the young athletes was a very good coach. Nobody said anything. [This occurred on team trips and at his home]. As expected, on team trips he was full of filthy jokes and sexist. It has been a long time since I found anything he does or says to be funny. (031:36F)

There is a paradox here in that a coach's work may be highly regarded even if he makes very poor moral choices. The athlete reporting the above is conflicted because on the one hand, she regards him as an excellent coach, and on the other, she refuses to participate in these presumably team-building experiences.

There are other more subtle forms of sexism that hinder the quality of athletes' experiences in sport. For example, two athletes identified the inappropriate and sexist attitudes of their coach and their male teammates as a problem:

> Not to be allowed to say anything because you're female or public arguments about girls not being capable of operating power tools to work on equipment or of operating a van. The coach and the male athletes concurred. (105:30F)

> The coach thought a billboard of a topless woman in Italy was something to be hooted at. He also encouraged male athletes to be sexist as well. He did this on team trips, in hotels and during our regular training. (237:20F)

Female athletes were subjected to a sport experience where they felt undervalued because they were female. The male coaches and athletes in the above cases specifically fostered this attitude.

Sexism does not only affect the female athletes. As one male athlete wrote, he did not know what to do about his coach who "bragged about how he used to rape females when he was in university" (193:26M).

We must ask whether coaches who make poor choices, such as those above, can continue to be regarded as good coaches. Such coaches are placing their personal preferences (e.g., "I like pornography," "I am sexist") ahead of the principle values of sport (e.g., athlete-centredness). The consequences of sexual harassment are negative for all athletes, compelling female athletes to "accept" or "live with" the discriminatory attitudes of their coaches and teammates and encouraging male athletes to adopt discriminatory attitudes and behaviours.

Same-Sex Harassment and Abuse
Our survey revealed a few examples of sexual harassment or abuse by male coaches of male athletes or by female coaches of female athletes. Of same-sex harassment and abuse amongst males, athletes report the following:

> One coach abused young boys, sometimes during our training session. (141:29M)

> The coach was a pedophile. On team trips and during regular training, he would invite athletes to his apartment or something

would happen in the change rooms or when we were staying at a hotel on the road. (190:23F)

A coach I knew was taken to court for abusing young male athletes, his own players, on team trips, during regular training and in private locations. He was taken to court and charges were dropped on the condition that he undergo psychiatric treatment. He hasn't coached in our sport since. (257:30F)

The first example is reported at the level of hearsay, the second and third are more direct accounts. While only a small proportion of sexual harassment and abuse appears to occur between males, these situations illustrate that a coach who is a pedophile has ready access to boys in sport. Other forms of abuse are also reported.

My coach physically abused his athletes during regular training. On many occasions, the coach pulled, hit, pulled hair, and pushed athletes into the walls. He would also verbally abuse the athletes emotionally. I have waited many years to answer a survey like this, wanting someone to know how dangerous the coach was during the time I trained in [name of hometown]. (244:28M)

Worth noting is the athlete's comment about waiting a long time to tell someone about the abuses. As with sexual harassment and abuse, the dome of silence exists over other forms of violence in sport, making the telling about it difficult.

Abuse of female athletes by female coaches is equally rare.

There was a lack of support or recognition by the NSO [National Sporting Organization] for the athletes' situation. It was ongoing between the female coach and her female athletes. During the 1980s a situation occurred between a coach and some athletes, all the same gender, that became inappropriate because of pressure placed on others to enter into similar situations. Selection to team was then compromised. (136:36M)

The account is a thinly veiled reference to lesbianism. The sexual harassment is seen to be "promotion of a lesbian lifestyle" in a way that "compromised team selection." Coaches must select athletes on the basis of their abilities and potential as performers, not for their sexual availability or sexual orientation, whether that orientation is heterosexual, homosexual or bisexual. Curiously, both reports above are made by male athletes.

"Coaches are maligned": The Response of Some Athletes to Sexual Harassment and Abuse

Despite the recognition of power and authority of coaches, some athletes believe that coaches are maligned and that athletes bear responsibility for sexual activity between a coach and athlete. These are strongly held opinions amongst a small minority of athletes. First, some believe that athletes pursue coaches and that it is the athletes who have sexual motives. Note the following:

> An athlete accused the coach and the coach lost his position. Yet all evidence indicated that athlete pursued the coach during training. The coach was married with three children. The athlete made advances to the coach but was turned down. She indicated she would "get" the coach since he would not respond to her advances. This occurred over a period of time and was not just an isolated incident. (013:34M)

There are other examples of athletes "pursuing" their coaches:

> On team trip at the hotel the coach and player had short relationship, slept together, then player claimed she was forced. (129:25F)

> The players blamed the coach for something they consented to and pushed to have happen [sexual contact]. As a result the coach was fired. The coach was blamed for something two players wanted and consented to happen. They then turned around and blamed the coach and as a result our sport lost one of the top coaches in the field. (148:25F)

In both cases, what is not in dispute is that the coaches had sex with the athletes. However, while we regard these as cases of sexual harassment and/or abuse, the athletes reporting them obviously see them differently. We would reiterate, since coaches and athletes in the coach-athlete relationship should decline having any sexual contact with each other and since it is the coach who is in a position of power over the athlete, it is unequivocally the coach's responsibility to not engage in sexual activity with the athlete.

The issue of false reporting is raised by one athlete, who writes:

> Was the response voluntary? Not in my heart. A sport coach was accused and reviled by his sport federation before they had received information about the situation. He was acquitted and

it is now known that the whole story was invented by some young girls who were jealous. That also happens in sport. (040:32F)

Given the level of evidence required in the complaint process, this is not an unusual verdict. It does not however indicate a false complaint, but an unproven one.

Coaches have a responsibility to "decline having any sexual contact with athletes" (Robertson 1997:5) for as long as they maintain the position of trust and authority and for as long afterwards as the remains of authority are present. To repeat, coaches who sexually harass and abuse athletes breach the trust in the coach-athlete relationship.

As Sheila Robertson writes, "a position of authority invokes notions of power and the ability to hold in one's hand the future or destiny of the person who is the object of the exercise of authority," and "the nature of the relationship between an adult and a young person is such that it creates an opportunity for all the persuasive and influencing factors which adults hold over young persons to come into play" (1997:5). Coaches who are mindful of this enormous responsibility have the potential to become excellent coaches. Others may become good technical coaches but can never fulfil the true promise inherent in the value-based sport system Canada is striving to create.

Athletes

Nine female and three male athletes report seeing or hearing about sexual harassment and abuse perpetrated by athletes. This is the second largest category of sexual harassment and abuse reports. In the first two examples, athletes are reported to have sexually assaulted women in the hotels in which they were staying.

> Rape done by athletes in my own sport at a hotel … on a trip some years ago, former members of my provincial team raped a maid of the hotel that the team was staying at. (008:20M)

> One female athlete was raped by the male players on a team from another country. The athletes got hungry late in the evening, went down to the hotel kitchen and on the way, found the young female athlete alone in the corridor. They raped her. (104:29F)

This is not a "boys will be boys" activity. It is more like the "wilding activity" reported in New York where a "pack of young men" assaulted a woman because they wanted something to do. We ask what these male athletes had been taught and how they were being supervised. When athletes travel together, they and their coaches have a responsibility to ensure responsible behaviour. These examples illustrate that it is not only athletes who are subjected to sexual predation but that others are also vulnerable.

A number of other examples provided by athletes involve the use of alcohol and the "team party" experience. When athletes get together for social reasons, the respect they have for each other should be evident. The depth to which it is sometimes lacking is evident in the following:

> An athlete had sex with another athlete at a party—the woman was passed out from too much alcohol. (128:28M)

> I was a victim of attempted sexual abuse at the age of fifteen by a twenty-one-year-old on a national-team trip. I had been drinking, we both had, and I had kissed him. Later he followed me to my hotel room and forced himself on me, pushing me to the floor with him on top of me. Fortunately my roommate came in and told him to leave. I told him to stop but he didn't. (237:20F)

> After a competition, we had a party at the hotel. We were a lot together in a small hotel room and before anyone knew what was happening, one of my teammates began to touch a female athlete on her naked skin and kiss her. He was very drunk. A little later, he forced her out of the room, forced himself on her and all the rest. It is not the first time that he did that either. (214:22M)

All three reports include sexual assault. In the first and second, no consent was given. Consent cannot be given if one is asleep or "passed out." The athlete in the second account was additionally vulnerable because she was fifteen years of age at the time and the person assaulting her was more than two years older. [23] In the third, alcohol was involved, the perpetrator had a history of similar assaults, and no one in the group tried to stop it. Their collective lack of action while they watched the assault begin and knew where it would lead is a measure of the sheer strength of the dome of silence over speaking out about sexual violence.

Athletes can also become obsessed with other athletes. Here is a report from an athlete with direct knowledge of a stalker.

> A teammate of mine was stalked by another obsessed teammate on team trips, during regular training and in hotels. One of my

teammates had a friendship which developed into a brief relationship. When it was called off, the other became obsessive;
stalking, dangerous and psychopathic. As a teammate and
friend, I got caught in the middle. (108:35F)

All of the accounts of sexual harassment and assault by athletes, we
believe, are testimony to the culture that exists in sport which pressures
male athletes to be hypersexual and to tolerate or even encourage this
in others. The sport context is a unique one and presents unusual opportunities for athletes to travel, to be unsupervised, to abuse alcohol
and to engage in inappropriate sexual activity. The fact that incidents of
sexual abuse and harassment by athletes are for the most part unreported remains problematic for sport and for all its participants.

Medical Doctors, Medical Personnel and Physiotherapists
Five athletes, three female and two male, report that they had seen or
heard of athletes being sexually harassed or abused by medical personnel. Additionally, three other female athletes report hearing about abuses
by physiotherapists. Almost all of these accounts are secondhand. Three
of the accounts involve physicians using their position to sexually harass women athletes at sport venues or in restaurants and bars. One of
these resulted in a charge being laid unsuccessfully. Two other reports
involve the drug testing situation where medical personnel supervise
the proceedings. One involves the previously mentioned testing incident at a World Cup competition where a man was sent into the bathroom to watch a female athlete provide a urine sample. Another concerns femininity testing where some female members of the Canadian
team were harassed by male officials who

> … ogled the athletes' genitals to verify if they were female. Some
> lewd comments were made. (042:35M)

Three female athletes report hearing about abuses by physiotherapists who had athletes remove clothing unnecessarily or who touched
athletes in ways that made them uncomfortable. For example, one athlete writes:

> One female athlete who had problems with sexual harassment
> by a physiotherapist who took advantage of the treatments, par-
> ticularly the massages. This happened both at the regular train-
> ing site and away on trips. The physio travelled with us. The
> physio would get the athlete to undress, something that was
> not necessary and then massage the athlete while she was lying

on her back. He touched her in ways that made her uncomfortable and made comments about her body. She told the other female athletes and after that, none of them wanted to go to see that physio. (036:25F)

Another athlete, writing about a long-drawn-out complaint process, indicates that:

> In the case of one of the physiotherapists, charges were laid. The review board agreed that the complainant was telling the truth, but did not revoke the licence of the offender. In his office, a friend of mine was sexually harassed—touched in an unacceptable way on the breast—when she was treated for a back injury. His defence was he had to touch her to treat her shoulder—which was never injured. For the appearance before the review board he created a whole file about a supposed shoulder problem. (145:27F)

These reports are disturbing because they seem to indicate a violation of the trust which is foundational to the professional-client relationship. Such experiences are likely to upset the athletes' trust "in a broader sense ... sometimes having lifelong repercussions" (Tomlinson and Strachan 1996:37).

Strangers

Some sexual harassment and abuse events happen at the hands of strangers. Five athletes, all female, report seeing or hearing of incidents where strangers approached athletes. In two cases, it was to take pictures and make lewd comments, as well as "calling, following, staring, touching while walking by, wanting us to go home with them." In two other cases, the strangers gained access to young athletes' bathroom facilities:

> In regular training, an athlete I knew was attacked while in the bathroom at her training facility. She however fought the guy off. She didn't know him. He was just someone in the public park. (068:16F)

> At an international competition in [a foreign country], one of my teammates, younger than me, was going to the bathroom and looked up to see a man peering into her stall. It was right before we competed. (082:17F)

The final report is of a violent sexual assault by a stranger of an athlete on her training run:

> She was attacked just a few steps from her apartment at the end of her training run. She was attacked and sexually assaulted from the back. He raped her with the aid of a knife. He cut up her vagina. She was almost dead from loss of blood. It happened on the street at dusk. (183:35F)

Athletes often train and perform in places which are open to the public; this can make them vulnerable to attack. The athlete in the third example was alone, was near death and fortunately was found in time to be treated for her physical injuries. The incidents indicate not only the need for better supervision for athletes at competition sites and during team trips, but for athletes to train in groups rather than singly. It would also help if they were able to avoid isolated locations. While there is no real way sport can prevent all sexual abuse from happening, it can certainly help athletes to adopt training patterns which reduce their risk.

National-team Committee Members
One female athlete reports problems with the provincial coaches and national-team committee members who wanted to sleep with athletes. The reported abuses happened on team trips, principally in the hotel in which the athletes were staying.

> All qualifying tournaments and the national-team championships ... many of the female athletes were pressured by some committee members and coaches to sleep with them to better their chances to get on the team. (234:24F)

This strikes at the heart of athletes' opportunities to make the national team and to be selected for various tours of competition. Only by getting through these narrow doors can athletes progress towards world championships in their sport. The coaches and selection committee members are in a clear conflict of interest if they engage in such activities. It compromises their judgement and makes a fallacy of the strict selection criteria developed in advance of such competitions. These sexual predators are using their positions of power to gain sexual access to athletes.

Managers
The last report is one athlete's account of apparent sexual harassment or abuse of athletes by a site manager. An official complaint was filed because

... of sexual harassment during one summer. It was during regular training and the site was a public place. We felt the manager of the training facility was touching and looking (gawking) at female athletes too much ... usually unwanted—always hugging and putting his arms around girls, also staring at them when they were in bathing suits, sports bras, etc., but he never did this to males. In most cases the women, in my and many other athletes' opinions, looked very uncomfortable. I wrote a letter to his boss, as did two other women after me. We were challenged on the validity of our charges, despite backing from coaches and other athletes, both male and female. (185:21F)

This kind of behaviour prevents athletes from being able to train or perform in a secure environment free from harassment. In other words, the quality of their experience is compromised by the unwanted sexual attention. It also illustrates again how difficult it is for all concerned to utilize the complaint processes.

Summary of What was Seen or Heard of Sexual Harassment or Abuse
Because of the sheer number of reports from athletes, we can comfortably assume that many athletes, particularly female athletes, are well aware of instances of sexual harassment and abuse. Although we asked what athletes had seen or heard, some provided accounts in which they were personally involved. Athletes wrote six times as many accounts involving coaches as involving others. Medical doctors or personnel, physiotherapists, strangers, national-team committee members and site managers are also implicated in these reports but in far fewer accounts. All accounts, no matter how minor, are essential to our understanding of how and under what conditions athletes are subjected to sexual violence.

Repeatedly, the issue of abuse of power by coaches and others in positions of authority over athletes is raised. Athletes see and hear much about harassment and abuse, seldom report it, and are frequently unhappy with the outcome of any complaints. We are left with the impression that those in positions of authority who have sexual motives have almost no difficulty in selecting vulnerable athletes upon whom to prey. Even when these behaviours occur in public, little is done to curtail these activities. The fact that sexual harassment and abuse experiences seem to be well known indicates the sheer size of this "open secret in sport" and the impunity with which coaches and others can be sexual predators.

The "blame the athlete" attitude by a few athletes is somewhat disturbing. It is important for all athletes to understand that these issues directly affect them, whether as victims or as participants in the chilly climate created by sexism in sport. It is athletes who are "in the know" about the nature and scope of the problem of sexual harassment and abuse. They are the ones with first-hand experience of the problem. Their voices must be strong and united if we are to eradicate these abuses from sport.

Finally, the gendered nature of sexual harassment and abuse could not be more evident. The great majority of reported incidents which athletes have seen or heard about in their sport or in other sports involves males in authority who are involved in the abuse of female athletes. However, the section on same-sex abuse is a cautious reminder that wherever there are vulnerable athletes, and whatever their sex or sexual orientation, there is the potential for sexual harassment and abuse. In essence, these results confirm that harassment and abuse are not secret but rather are apparent to many, including athletes, who cannot or will not speak out. Is it apathy on the part of the athletes or is it that they fear the consequences of speaking out?

ATHLETES' EXPERIENCES WITH SEXUAL HARASSMENT IN THE SPORTING CONTEXT

Here, we asked athletes to share their personal histories of sexual harassment and abuse and to describe the situations which upset them the most. Many had already provided first person accounts in other sections of the survey and we include here only those accounts which portray new situations.

Put-downs and Insults

Many athletes responding to the survey report experiencing put-downs or insults based on their being female or gay or for some other reason or characteristic (N=107). These put-downs or insults are equally likely to come from coaches (37.2 percent) as from other athletes (37 percent), and 54.7 percent of female athletes and 29.1 percent of male athletes experience them as serious enough to cause distress (see Figure 5). Female athletes are more likely to be upset if the comment is made by a coach rather than by teammates or some other person in the sporting context. The gendered nature of how put-downs are experienced is significant (p.<006). This is testimony to the effect coaches can have on athletes, particularly male coaches on female athletes, where the communication is both negative and a cross-gendered put-down. Further, the female athletes are more likely than male athletes to experience such put-downs from their coaches, while male athletes are more likely to hear them from other athletes.

We find it disturbing that when athletes were asked how they dealt

Figure 5: How Much do Insults Hurt?

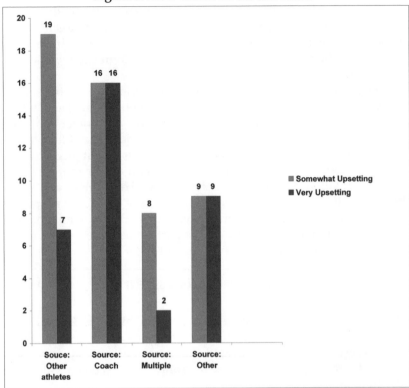

with the put-downs, no discernible strategy emerged. Responses varied from doing nothing or making excuses, to avoiding the person, going along with what the person said, confronting the person, getting angry or some combination of these. Clearly, if the person making the insult or put-down is a coach or another athlete, a number of the strategies would be difficult to carry out. We will see that this lack of understanding or co-ordination of actions after upsetting experiences repeats itself when athletes are confronted with other forms of sexual harassment/abuse.

Sexually Suggestive Comments

Twenty-eight percent of athletes (N=75) report that in a sporting situation, someone made sexually suggestive comments about the athlete or his/her body. Interestingly, age and fear are not significant indicators of whether athletes receive such comments. However, gender is a significant indicator, with 42.6 percent of all females and only 10.3 percent of all males being made uncomfortable by such comments (p.<000).

Who makes these comments? Males are responsible for 81.3 percent of such comments and direct the huge majority of sexually suggestive comments towards females (p.<000). Again, there is no age group of athletes most vulnerable to such comments. We see the following pattern emerge:

Table 9: Sexually Suggestive Comments

Comments from ...	Comments to ...
Males	58 Female Athletes (83%)
Males	3 Male Athletes (4%)
Females	7 Male Athletes (10%)
Females	2 Female Athletes (3%)

In Table 9, we see 65 opposite-sex (93 percent) and 5 same-sex sexually suggestive comments (7 percent). Not surprisingly, this suggests that the great majority of sexual harassment of this type, 93 percent, is from one sex to another and that same-sex harassment is minimal. [24] Some comments are enough to make athletes afraid and gender is again a significant indicator of that fear (p.<005). Of the 75 athletes receiving sexually suggestive comments, 12 felt afraid afterwards: 11 females and 1 male.

One of the best contra-indicators for being victimized by sexually suggestive comments is income—the higher their income, the less likely it is that athletes will experience sexually suggestive comments which upset them. Athletes making less than $10,000 received 63.5 percent of such comments, compared to only 13.5 percent for those making $30,000 or more (p.<07).

Although 75 athletes report experiencing sexually suggestive comments which made them uncomfortable and 12 of those were afraid afterwards, there is again no clear strategy or strategies visible for how athletes dealt with this.

Fear
Athletes were asked whether an authority figure in a sporting situation had ever made them afraid by being sexually interested in them. Six and a half percent, or 17 athletes, responded positively, 15 women and 2 men. The authority figures were always male. Of those 17 athletes, 3 (1 female and 2 male) report actually having sex with the person because of fear. Two others, both female, had sex with the person due to the particular fear of losing their place on the team. Here we have evidence of 5 athletes who were made afraid because of unwanted sexual attention from male authority figures and, because of that fear, had sexual intercourse with those authority figures.

These people in positions of authority have abused the trust given to them by the sport system and by the athletes, and used their positions both to create a level of fear in athletes and to gain sexual access to those athletes based on the presence of that fear. Coaches and others must be expected not to cross the line between responsible behaviour and such abuse of authority.

Sex with a Person in a Position of Authority

Perhaps the most damning information to come from this study is the fact that more than 1 in 5 athletes has had sex with a person in a position of authority over them in the sport context. In a question about sex with authority figures in sport (though not due to fear), 58 athletes, that is, 21.8 percent, indicated that they had experienced sexual intercourse with such persons. Forty-eight of the authority figures were older than the athletes; some were much older. Four athletes reported age differences of more than twenty years between themselves and the authority figure with whom they had sex. The majority of those subjected to sex with authority figures are female; the majority of the authority figures having sex with their athletes are male.

An equally disturbing feature here is that of those 58 athletes, 15 of them (26 percent, 11 female and 4 male) also reported being insulted, ridiculed, made to feel like a bad person, or slapped, hit, punched or beaten by these authority figures. The persons in positions of authority were most often identified as coaches, although the group includes physiotherapists, medical doctors, athletic trainers and so on. This sharply "raises the red flag" about authority figures having sex with and being sexually abusive to athletes, some of them very young. We must also be concerned that one-quarter of these authority figures resort to additional physical and/or emotional abuse.

Once again, we underline the importance of the issue of consent. If one person is in a position of authority over another, the other cannot give consent. Consent is simply not possible in such circumstances (Brackenridge and Kirby 1999). It is also not a defence for the person in a position of authority to say that the athlete "came on to him/her" or that the two were looking for a long-term relationship ending in marriage. It is a conflict of interest and, some would say, a betrayal of fiduciary trust (Levine 1996)[25] for a person in authority over another to use that position to gain sexual access. Even if the athlete and the person in authority over the athlete are adults, the Code of Ethics for coaches prohibits such activity until the person in authority has been out of the sphere of influence (power) over the athlete for a substantial period of time. Sport organizations will have to work very hard to eliminate the abuses of authority such as these apparent in our findings.

UNWANTED SEXUAL EXPERIENCES IN THE SPORTING CONTEXT

Poisoned Environment/Chilly Climate of Sport

Twenty-eight female and ten male athletes described a variety of behaviours which together contribute to the poisoned environment of sport. Not surprisingly, much of the sexual harassment of athletes is about name-calling. The athletes, most of them female, are targets for comments which betray sexist, homophobic and ageist attitudes in others in sport. Some of the name-calling is not regarded by the athletes as particularly serious, although there are indications that some realize it is a slippery slope into other forms of harassment or abuse. For example:

> It varied. Nothing serious enough to be the "most" upsetting—just constant comments re: issues of attractiveness, looking feminine, being flat-chested, good or bad in bed because of being an athlete, etc. (011:34F)

Females are four times more likely than are males to report insults of a sexual nature as being upsetting. The harassment comes from all sides. It includes insults, use of sexist and demeaning language, use of particular words to create a lack of comfort, vulgarity, and physical touching in sexual ways. Sometimes the comments weren't meant in an abusive manner. At other times, the put-downs are vulgar, sexist and demeaning to women athletes or sexually insulting to a particular athlete:

> My male team members made up nicknames for all the females that were sexually insulting. Every time I went somewhere I would often hear my initials which would stand for something else. I heard from one of the other women what they stand for! I joked about it, let them know I knew what they were talking about. (180:24F)

Some male athletes also experience sexism or insulting remarks, although it is far less frequent an occurrence:

> I was upset by what I saw as male bashing by females. I was most upset by "sexually inferior comments." (161:20M)

> As a man I don't enjoy having a woman shout out cutting remarks, especially when they don't know me. Coming from another man isn't fun either, just let me play as hard as I can. Isn't that what fair sportsmanship is all about? (189:34M)

Some of this harassment is explicitly sexual in nature, for example, comments in a sexual way on the physical characteristics of the athletes. Other forms of harassment are more subtle, for example, the use of demeaning language or profanity to "put down" the athletes. When harassment comes from other athletes, it is indicative of the pervasiveness and tolerance of sexual violence in the sporting environment.

The environment of sexism can be established and perpetrated by both athletes and coaches. See the following:

> Sexual harassment—athletes commenting on how female athletes look and using sexual jokes. Coaches making comments and advances towards athletes. I have seen coaches within my own sport take advantage of young athletes on their own. I have heard and seen male athletes leering and commenting on the physical features of women athletes, like in respect to the size of their chests, how tight her ass is, etc. (199:22F)

> Coach and other athletes make these comments, ... being called a "slut" or when people make jokes about women as a group, etc. I avoid these people when I can, sometimes I go along with what the person said, confront the person or get angry. (237:20F)

Harassment coming from a number of people concurrently provides strong evidence of the sexist climate in sport and the active participation of athletes and coaches, particularly males, in actively maintaining that climate. It appears to be based on a "sense of superiority": of the male athlete and of the male person in sport. It is all too easy for those with sexist attitudes to see female athletes as second-class citizens and as sexual objects. Some female athletes just consider it part of the sport experience, for example:

> The coach harasses me all the time. My sport is male dominated so I am used to it. (119:25F)

Most athletes want to be treated with respect and are conscious of the particular responsibilities a coach has for establishing fairness and respect in the training environment. They do not like being on the receiving end of harassments which include the use of profanity and insulting words or phrases, nor do they like to see others harassed:

> I don't like male coaches using profane language just to be cool. It was uncalled for and the person who said it is supposed to be a role model and he said it in a public place. (117:22F)

I've been called everything by my coach. "Bitch," "easy," things like "pussy-sets," "come on now, be a man," "show some balls." Real sexism. (111:21F)

Coaches, teammates, parents and friends all use it. A head coach, I found out, had commented on the size of my breasts. This deeply hurt me as I felt that the coach regarded me as an athlete when in fact, he looked at me as a pair of "chugs." I began to be very self-conscious of my breast size, which still occurs today. (230:26F)

When harassing behaviour comes from the coach, a poor standard is set. Also, as we have shown, such behaviour from the coach has a greater negative impact on the athletes than if it comes from others in sport:

The coach upset me the most because a reference was made to me that I was a pussy and an easy target for sexual gratification. (199:22F)

The gendered nature of the harassment is evident. There are other examples of sexual harassment involving insults. They include the "trash talk" of male referees, the sexist attitudes of "foreign" coaches, officials, and managers, ageist discrimination by the president of the provincial or territorial sport association, and sexist behaviour of club and touring professionals.

The Poisoned Environment/Chilly Climate for Gays and Lesbians
Homophobia is a fear of homosexuals or homosexuality. In our study it has taken the form of labelling athletes as homosexual as a way of putting them down. Although the numbers are small, roughly equal numbers of females and males report this form of harassment. Curiously enough, the actual sexual identity of athletes does not seem to be the issue when homophobia is expressed. Intolerance is expressed towards individuals independent of whether they are actually lesbian or gay or sometimes if they are just presumed to be homosexual. First, when women excel in sport, they sometimes suffer a form of harassment which calls into question their femininity or even their sexuality. Here are four examples.

I was called a dyke basically because I was athletic. (108:35F)

A male athlete accused me and a female co-athlete of being sexually involved for the reason that we were spending a lot of time together to avoid the abusive and negative treatment by the temporary coach and some of the male athletes. (105:30F)

The coach called me a lesbian in front of the other athletes, because I am. This was upsetting because I am not "out."200:36F)

The allusions to my sexuality are humiliating and I have made a great effort to show that they don't affect me. I have developed the "le dos de canard ..." [the back of a duck]. So, when the president of my club made an allusion to my sexuality and said that I wasn't normal, it really upset me. It is not that I was really perturbed, but I know I don't have as much confidence. (031:36F)

In the first and second examples, women are labelled lesbians simply because they excel in sport or spend a lot of time with other female athletes. In the third, the coach actually broke a confidence with the athlete, "outing" her against her wishes and putting her at some risk. In the fourth, the athlete's confidence was lowered because of continuing harassment from her coach and the club president about her sexual orientation.

Male athletes in some sports also experience homophobic comments, particularly when they excel in sports dominated by females:

Other athletes called me a "faggot." It was not very upsetting, especially since I live with my girlfriend. However, it is upsetting because it continues to go on. (202:28M)

As I got older, my athleticism excelled, so did the coach's comments about my sexuality. I remember [coaches' names] commented all the time about such faggots as myself. To think I won these national and international medals. I did nothing, ignored it in silence. Then I got angry! (244:28M)

The homophobia of the perpetrators of such discrimination is evident. Human rights legislation in Canada protects individuals from discrimination against them because of their membership or perceived membership in certain groups. If such discrimination results in these athletes receiving lesser services, housing or employment, they may actually have some recourse through their provincial human rights commission.

What did athletes do about these various harassments? Some ignored it and did nothing. Others laughed it off or got angry. One person focused on his performance task:

> The sexually harassing comments didn't upset me because it was all in the name of sport by trying to upset me and get me off my "game mode." I did nothing, ignored it. (241:31M)

As with victims in other forms of harassment, where a complaint process is needed to initiate some form of solution, the athletes are reluctant even to begin the complaint process. Athletes' reluctance existed whether the complaint process was housed inside or outside the sport system. They find it easier in most cases to ignore the abuse and/ or its source. There is no apparent mechanism readily available to athletes to stop these forms of harassment, which demean them and have a negative effect on the quality of their sport experience.

OTHER UNWANTED SEXUAL EXPERIENCES IN THE SPORTING CONTEXT
Here, we determined what other unwanted sexual experiences athletes had had. We also addressed the specific question about what kinds of unwanted sexual experiences athletes had prior to the age of sixteen years, the age of consent in many provinces.

Obscene Phone Calls
Obscene phone calls from someone they have known through sports are reported by 4.1 percent of athletes. Age and gender[26] are important predictors of whether this will occur—athletes over twenty-one years of age and female are the most likely to receive these calls.

Sexual Comments or Advances
Fifty-one athletes (19.2 percent) complained of upsetting sexual comments or advances in the sporting context. Gender is again an important predictor (p.<000). Many more females than males experience such comments. Males made 82.4 percent of these comments, and 90 percent of these comments were directed towards females.

Stalking
Athletes report being stalked on training runs if they are alone, in corridors of training centres if they have a regular pattern of activity and when they are at home.Thirteen female and 4 male athletes, 6.4 percent, report being followed or stalked in the sporting context. Older athletes are more likely to report this experience.[27] The stalker was always of the opposite sex.

Pinching or Rubbing of an Athlete, in a Public Place,
against the Athlete's Will
Fourteen percent, 37 athletes, report experiencing a situation which upset then when someone pinched them or rubbed against their body, in a
public place, against their will. Gender is significant (p.<004) in who
experienced these activities and in who does the pinching or rubbing.
Thirty-two of the incidents were done to athletes of the opposite sex.
Another five incidents involved males pinching or rubbing male athletes. None were reported between women.

Before and after Sixteen: Flashing
Flashing is the exposure of one's genitals in public, and in our study, 3.2
percent or 8 athletes report that before they were sixteen years of age,
they had been upset by a "flasher" in a sporting context. Only 1 of the 8
athletes was male. The flasher was male in all but one case. An equal
number of athletes, but this time all female, report being upset by a
flasher when they were sixteen years of age or older. The flasher was
male in 6 of the 8 cases, female in 1 and unidentified in 1. A total of 16
athletes, 14 female, have been upset by these experiences in a sporting
context. The flasher was identified as male in 13 of 16 cases.

Before and after Sixteen:
Forced Sexual Intercourse (Oral, Vaginal or Anal)
Forced sexual intercourse is a problem in sport. Attempted or successful forced sexual intercourse while they were younger than sixteen is
reported by 2 females and 3 males. These athletes were sexually assaulted. When describing the situation which upset them most, 4 of the
5 described experiencing rape or attempted rape by males. One male
athlete reports being raped by a female. Also, in 4 of the 5 cases, the
perpetrator was 5 to 20 years older than the younger athlete.

An additional 14 females and 4 males report experiencing attempted
or forced sexual intercourse when they were sixteen and older. When
reporting the situation which was the most upsetting for them, the females all describe being raped or experiencing attempted rape by males.
Three of the 4 males report being raped or experiencing attempted rape
by females. Gender of the athlete and gender of the perpetrator[28] are
significantly related, with the perpetrator being of the opposite sex in
all but one reported case. Age is an important indicator for the perpetrator, with the perpetrator being 5 to 27 years older than the athlete in
8 of the 18 cases. The age differences between athletes and perpetrators
is a significant one and perhaps signals that athletes are safer with persons their own age.

In total, 23 of 266 athletes (8.6 percent) report having experienced forced sexual intercourse or attempted forced sexual intercourse in the sporting context. These occur in many places: at the sport site, before or after sport training, on the way to and from training, at social events organized for sport, on team trips and in the perpetrators' or athletes' homes. When we combine the 23 athletes who report having experienced rape or attempted rape with the 58 athletes who reported having sex with a person in a position of authority, a total of 81 athletes (30.5 percent) have experienced these kinds of sexual abuse at the hands of persons, usually male, who are older than themselves, sometimes much older. Organizing of athlete safety during sport training and competitions needs to be re-evaluated in light of these facts.

Unwanted Sexual Touching of Athletes under Age Sixteen
Six females and 1 male report some form of sexual touching of their genitals, grabbing or kissing or feeling or some combination of these, before the athletes reached sixteen years of age. Two also report receiving sexual comments. In all but one case, the perpetrator was male.

Rape, Sexual Assault or Attempted Rape or Sexual Assault
in a Sporting Context
We asked a final, catch-all question to get at other information about both attempted and completed rapes and sexual assaults.[29] Of all the athletes who responded to the questionnaire, 13 athletes (or 5 percent, 12 of them female) report their experiences in answer to this question. The perpetrators were identified as male in 11 cases and unidentified in 2. Age of the athlete is not a significant predictor of this; all athletes are vulnerable. However the age difference between the athlete and the perpetrator is significant, again with the perpetrator being older than the athlete in the 8 of 13 cases. We note that in 2 cases, the perpetrators were 25 and 32 years older than the athletes.

Most of the athletes, 11 of 13, sought some sort of help afterwards. Again, no definite strategy is evident, as athletes approached a variety of people. Eight found the help they received useful, 3 did not. In 2 cases, criminal charges were pressed. In 3, more informal procedures were initiated. Consequences for athletes experiencing rape, sexual assault or attempted rape include changing teams, quitting sport, changing personal behaviour or some combination of these.

Our figure of 5 percent in this final category does not agree with the actual incidences reported for sex with persons in a position of authority and forced sexual intercourse or attempted forced sexual intercourse. What this shows is that, although athletes can clearly describe what they have seen, heard and experienced, they may not fully understand the legal labelling of these events as sexual harassment and assault .

This may explain why many athletes might say, "No, I have not been sexually harassed or abused," but then go on to say "but this happened to me and it made me feel uncomfortable or abused."

And Should I Complain?

When we asked what athletes had done afterwards, we found that few assaults or attempted assaults were followed up with an official complaint, and even when a complaint was made, the athletes were unlikely to have been satisfied with the process and the outcome for the perpetrator.

Sexual Assault Followed by Official Complaint

Those who sexually assault athletes appear to be able to do so with relative impunity since few complaints are laid. Provided here are four examples where athletes actually chose the difficult path of laying an official complaint. The first is the account of an athlete who laid a complaint against a therapist:

> I was sexually harassed and assaulted. There was nowhere to go for help. I eventually filed a complaint. He was found not guilty for lack of evidence. I could have used some help. Both mentally and financially. It is now in process of appeal. He was forty-eight and I was twenty-three. It happened in his office during a therapy session. I was assaulted once, sexually harassed several times. Like he made several harassing comments about how I owed him, about sexual activity, and about running away to Hawaii together. Eventually felt my breasts and inner thighs. I never returned to the office. (049:23F)

In the second, we are unsure who the harasser is, but the athlete is clearly frightened and is unsatisfied with the result of the complaint:

> Only harassment, no sex ... my employer investigated and warned the accused, informed him of appropriate behaviour for his position. The accused found out who made complaint; threatened retaliation against my coach. He claimed my coach was out to ruin him; cornered teammate who also wrote letter and then he claimed our coach forced her to write it and that she wanted him fired; just gave me evil looks, making it difficult to focus on training; then approached me saying I must have misinterpreted his behaviour and he wanted to be friends. I am unsatisfied with results of this complaint. I went out of my way to avoid him; wouldn't wear a bathing suit, etc., at the

training facility. I felt extremely uncomfortable when he was around and had difficulty training in his presence. (185:21F)

In the next two examples, the assailant was another athlete's parent and a boyfriend respectively. In both cases, the athlete initiated the complaint process.

In August [year provided], he was about fifty and another athlete's parent. I was seventeen. It happened in this man's home. I had gone to his home to pick up a knapsack which belonged to his son. It only happened once. He was touching my bum, slapping my face, kissing my mouth and neck, making me wash dishes, sit and lie on certain beds and chairs, eat food that was presented to me, making sexual comments to me. Afterwards, I needed psychotherapy and counselling, I lost interest in sport and changed my behaviour in sporting situations. I am no longer optimistic about common difficulties everyone has in the training cycle. Criminal charges and civil actions resulted and there was an investigation by police. After a court hearing found him guilty, he was sent to prison and later got probation. I was satisfied. (127:20F)

I [was] raped in April [year provided] by one of the club players. He was twenty-nine. I was thirty-three. It occurred in my home. He wanted sex. I didn't and said so. It happened once as far as I know. Fondling, penetration but then I blacked out during penetration. He also wanted oral sex before penetration. I told a friend, a minister and the police. I laid criminal charges and there was an investigation by the police. He was found not guilty by the court in June [year provided] due to evidence he stated concerning events I have no memory of during the blackout. I am unsatisfied with the results. I had to retire from my paid work due to PTSD [post-traumatic stress disorder] caused by the rape, had to spend time in a provincial mental institution for suicidal depression brought on by the rape incidents and flashbacks to childhood assaults. (256:36F)

Not only are the accounts alarming, but the lack of satisfaction of the complainants is disturbing. Only 1 of the 4 complainants is satisfied and 2 are unsatisfied with the results of the complaint process. One complaint process in still in appeal. Lack of evidence is cited as the reason for the "not guilty" outcome in 2 of the 4 examples. All the athletes still have a great deal of difficulty with the after-effects, some using an extensive counselling process, others changing their behaviour so that they will not encounter the accused perpetrators. For the athlete in the last example, the sexual assault started a long process of recovered memories about unwanted sex with one of her parents and the counselling was lifesaving. Note the considerable amount of support each athlete needs to make a complaint and to deal with the effects of such assaults.

Sexual Assault Not Followed by Official Complaint
In this section are reports of numerous sexual assaults on athletes that have not resulted in a complaint being made. In each case, the assault is reported to have occurred only once and the athlete did nothing about it through official channels. For example, one athlete reports:

> Three years ago, it happened to me, at the coach's house. He was six years older than me. He made sexually explicit comments that made me feel unsafe and he felt me, grabbed me and kissed me. The sexual assault, it only happened once. (197:19F)

Another writes about her fear:

> I had an unwanted sexual experience with someone who was both a teacher and a coach. I lost some of my opportunities in sport because I lost my team place. Afterwards, I changed my behaviour in sporting situations and I tried to avoid the coach. I was afraid and I couldn't concentrate on training anymore. (131:22F)

Two more athletes write about unwanted sexual experiences with their coaches. In one, the athlete made considerable efforts after the event to avoid the coach:

> I had an unwanted sexual experience with my coach. He was also a family member and friend. I sought help but it was not helpful and no actions against perpetrator were taken. As an athlete, I was always hoping I wouldn't run into him, avoiding him. In my case, everyone knew what was going on but no one would ever come forward. He was always protected. The solution is to make it easier to come forward. (184:21F)

> A male coach was always commenting on my looks and caressing my shoulders. He was eighteen. I was seventeen. We were

both at a sports centre in [a foreign country]. The sexual advances happened only once. He tried to have sexual intercourse with me when I had refused. (131:23F)

And another athlete reports on the breach of trust she felt when the coach, fifteen years older than her, invited her to his hotel room for an "individual meeting" prior to competition and used the occasion, and others like it, to sexually pursue her.

Cases of same-sex assault are also reported. One involved a Canadian coach and a player from another country's team and is reported by a Canadian athlete affected by the interaction.

I had a coach [a woman] go to bed with a female athlete who played on [another country's] team. An underage female on the team was with the coach until the coach asked that player to leave for an intimate moment. I thought this was in poor taste. The coach, in general, lacked respect for players and was a poor role model. (066:35F)

The degree of control a coach can have over an athlete is apparent in the reports. These are inappropriate behaviours for coaches, yet none of the athletes affected by the behaviour laid a complaint. As the athletes suggest, the risks are great, everything from feeling uncomfortable at future training to losing one's place on the national team to quitting sport.

As stated earlier, although 21.8 percent of athletes surveyed report having sexual intercourse with persons in positions of authority, they do not generally report these or see them as sexual assaults. Since these most often involve coaches, it signals to us the desperate need for education programs with athletes on sexual harassment and assault.

A number of sexual assaults not followed by a complaint from the victimized athlete were perpetrated by people the athletes knew well and trusted like family. In the first three examples, the perpetrator was another athlete, six or more years older than the victim, in the next, the perpetrator was an older friend of the family, and in the last example, the perpetrator was the athlete's date. In each case, the victim was female.

I was twenty, he was thirty-four. At a training camp, after the training in the evening, only once, he forced himself on me. After that I trained only with others present. (200:36F)

A male athlete on another team forced me. I was eighteen and he was twenty-six. It was in an hotel room after the champion-ship competition. There was drinking involved. It was sexual intercourse from behind. I was basically asleep. I told no one. (259:23F)

I was fifteen, he was twenty-one years old and it happened at the World Championships. Both of us were drunk. We had kissed and then we went back to the residence. I said goodbye but he followed me and forced me. I told him to stop. (237:20F)

This introduces a whole new dynamic into our understanding of sexual harassment and abuse. Fellow athletes are like family and, as such, should be safe confidants and supports. However, we find that fellow athletes on the same team can also put an athlete, particularly a female althlete, at great risk. Also in the "family" dynamic, a single account of an assault by a friend of the athlete's parents is provided:

When I was in my early twenties, one of my parents' male friends made a move towards me. We were playing Nintendo and he undid my bra. My parents and his wife were in the kitchen. I left the situation and went and slept on the couch in the den. He went back to where my parents were but came several times to kiss me on the cheek since I was turned sideways. I was shocked and told my parents the next day. This never happened again. (133:30F)

In the last example, sexual assault is responsible for breaking of the trust between an athlete and her date. This is date-rape:

He was not an athlete, but I was. I was fifteen and he was seventeen. It happened in a car on a date. I blamed myself for four years. I felt it was my fault for allowing myself to be in that situation. I wanted to fool around but I didn't want to have intercourse. Not telling anyone and blaming myself for those years really had an effect on my self-esteem. Even today after some counselling, I have low self-esteem. (207:25F)

Another sexual assault not resulting in a complaint being laid occurred where the assailant was a complete stranger, the assault occurred once and the athlete was left "without proof":

A male, I don't know his age, assaulted me in the summer. It happened at the local training facility. I was training alone. It was 8 p.m. and it happened once. I was approached by a stranger who began asking me questions about training, then quickly grabbed at my genital area. (052:23M)

This is one of the few accounts of a male sexual assault on another male. Our survey indicates that sexual assaults occur considerably more frequently from males to females and are rarely either same-sex or from females to males. However, we also suspect that considerable under-reporting exists in same-sex harassment.

In conclusion, an overwhelming number of athletes reporting sexual harassment and assault, including those reported in the statistical section of the chapter, do not begin a complaint process, for whatever reasons, against the perpetrators. It may be that the athletes simply do not have faith in the complaint processes. More likely however is that athletes have far too much to risk and, when they weigh the risks against the benefits of revealing these abuses, choose to be silent. There is undoubtedly pressure from authority figures in sport, including the coaches, for athletes not to "rock the boat" if they wish to continue to be successful. Combined with the tolerance of sexism and of sexual harassment, the lack of reporting on sexual assaults suggests that sport actively condones such behaviours.

Personal Consequences of these Events

Outcomes for the athletes who were victimized by sexual assault or attempted sexual assault are serious in both the short and the long-term. For many, it changed how they behaved in sport and in their day-to-day lives. Athletes found ways to take care of themselves by not associating with the perpetrators, by changing the training routine, by changing personal behaviour to become more professional, or by changing the situation or location so they would be less at risk. Several athletes continue to have long-term personal problems. They sought psychotherapy/counselling, refused media interviews, lost interest in sport and/or remained unable to deal with the experience and are now "violent and temperamental." One athlete simply responded: "Me, I fixed the problem myself" (173 32M).

What is surprising is the sense that the athletes are suffering through the experience alone, without the assistance of other athletes, their team or sport organization. There seems to be no connection between these athletes and the kinds of community supports—battered women's shelters, sexual assault organizations, and women's and men's groups— available to those outside of sport who have been victimized by sexual violence. Although we have a better understanding of what athletes experience in sport, we still do not really know what kind of support victimized athletes need and what is currently available to them. There is, however, no evidence that victimized athletes are advocating for systemic changes or assisting others to avoid such experiences.

CONCLUSION

In the first ever survey of current and recently retired national-team athletes in Canada, we have found that sexual harassment and abuse are indeed serious problems in sport. Results of the study show that sexual harassment and abuse are systemic problems that will need the combined efforts of athletes, sport organizations and governments to eradicate. This is the challenge for the sport community and for those who care about sport and our athletes: to lift the dome of silence surrounding the issue, to face the issue head-on and to end the abuse.

Both males and females are victimized, although athletes are much more aware of the victimization of women. As has been found in other studies, females are much more likely to be harassed or abused, and it is mostly males who are the perpetrators. Our statistics confirm what has been anecdotally known by many in sport for years. These reports are extremely disturbing, revealing patterns of systematic sexual harassment and abuse of athletes, often by authority figures. Our study points to the necessity for further investigation of this issue on a sport by sport basis and at all levels of sport competition.

Although sexual harassment/abuse is often seen as an issue for girls and women, it also concerns boys and men. The harasser is most often male, the victim most often female. However, there may be harassment by a member of the same sex, or a female harassing a male. The harassment can happen on the playing fields, tracks, rinks, pools or waterways. It can happen in change rooms, on buses, in cars, in hotel rooms and in elevators. It can occur on team trips or training courses, at conferences or team parties. It can happen to any member of the public using sport facilities or any member of a sport organization before, during, or after the regular sport participation. It usually happens repeatedly over a short or long period of time. Most often, it happens in private. Not only does sexual violence diminish the quality of sport performance but it negatively affects the quality of the experience for all concerned; the athletes, coaches, administrators and officials alike.

It has never been more clear that athletes need to be educated from a very young age about their right to enjoy sport free of sexual harassment and abuse. Education which gives them skills in recognizing such discriminations is an important step towards eradicating these from sport. Athletes talk of being uncertain of what supports are around them and of what processes are available to deal with harassment and abuse. Some talk about the process working in ways which actually undermine their complaints and where results or findings show the complaints to be "unsubstantiated." Athletes write about being maligned after the complaint process is over. It is clear that opportunities for change are minimized in such a climate. In sport, we are at a very preliminary point in creating processes to handle complaints and in communicating these to the athletes. Athletes do not want to be rape crisis counsellors—yet find themselves in this role when their friends and/or teammates turn to them for support.

Canada has positioned itself as a world leader in defending the human rights of oppressed peoples. In sport, this leadership is evident in the movements for accessible, drug-free and gender equitable sport. At the same time, the harassment of athletes, and in particular, sexual harassment/abuse, is a critical issue preventing quality sport experience for some participants.

NOTES

1. In this chapter, we present the results of our 1996 survey of Canadian current and recently retired (within the last five years) national-team athletes (Kirby and Greaves 1996). The survey instrument developed for this study was informed by a number of models, particularly the survey used in The Women's Safety Project by M. Randall and L. Haskell, (1995), noted in Canadian Panel on Violence Against Women (1993:A-A5).

2. For press coverage of the Graham James story, see the *Winnipeg Free Press*, January 4, 1997:1, the *Globe and Mail*, January 14, 1997: A1, and the *Gazette*, January 11, 1997, p. A16. For coverage on Graham Smith, see the *Edmonton Journal*, Dec. 1, 1993, A1. For coverage on Paul Hickson and Thomas Hamilton see Brackenridge 1996.

3. We would like to thank Sport Canada for their support of this research through the Applied Sport Research Program.

4. As Brackenridge (1997c) indicates, making sense of the definitions, for athletes and coaches, for the media, for legal and policy analysts and for new researchers into the field continues to be difficult because of the relativity of the existing data.

5. Note that more detailed information about the method of analysis is in Kirby and Greaves 1997.

6. Kirby and LeRougetel (1992) showed that females, on average, occupy on average only 30 to 35 percent of international, multi-sport teams (e.g., Olympic Games, Pan-American Games, Commonwealth Games, Para-Olympic Games).

7. The mean difference between current and retired athletes' salaries was 26.4 percent ($p<.000$).

8. Canada Census (1991) reports that in Canada, among those persons 15 years or older, 10 percent of females compared to 13 percent of males have university degrees. Females have a greater probability than males of having acquired other forms of certification or training at the post-secondary level (Statistique Canada 1995).

9. There has been some research which suggests that female athletes in some countries actually reach puberty later than their non-sport peers (Brackenridge and Kirby 1997). On average, although female athletes as a group experience puberty prior to male athletes, they become sexually active at an older age than male athletes.

10. Age is a significant predictor of sexual activity, significant at p. <.001 and those with lower incomes are more likely to be involved with only one person than those who have higher incomes (p. <.05). A multivariate analysis of age, income and sexual activity reveals that lower income athletes become sexually active at younger ages (2 as young as 8 years of age) than do higher income athletes.

11. The majority, 72 percent, were involved with only one partner. The others were involved with more than one person and were more likely to be involved with athletes on other teams rather than on their own team (p.<.000).

12. Gender predicts awareness of the issue among athletes (p.<.018). Not surprisingly, female athletes are much more likely than males to think these are issues, 62.1 percent and 37.9 percent respectively.

13. There is also a high degree of consistency between the number of affirmative answers to the question "does something need to be done about these issues in sport?" and "do you think these are issues in sport?" (81.2 percent and 80.5 percent respectively; p. <.000). Gender continues to be a significant predictor of whether athletes think action needs to be taken on issues (p.< .001), with females again more likely than males to think these are issues and that action needs to be taken.

14. Of those who feel less than very safe, 24.8 percent feel somewhat safe, 4.2 percent feel somewhat unsafe and 0.4 percent feel very unsafe.

15. The other 53.8 percent either did not respond to the question or did not know.

16. As Tomlinson and Strachan write, "Acting with respect for participants means that coaches do not make some participants more or less worthy as persons than others on the basis of gender, race, place of origin, athletic potential, colour, sexual orientation, religion, political beliefs, socioeconomic status, marital status, age, or any other conditions" (1996: 93).

17. In Canada, it is illegal to sexually interfere or sexually touch a child, to expose a child to bestiality or to expose one's genitals to a child, and a child cannot, under any conditions, give consent to such activities. Also, if a person is under fourteen years of age, special provisions for criminal charges for sexual assault exist. For those fourteen years of age but under eighteen, no consent can be given where sexual exploitation or assault causing bodily harm, including sexual assault, are present (Kirby and Brackenridge 1997; Casswell 1996).

18. Two reports from the College of Physicians and Surgeons of Ontario (1991a and b) illustrate the efforts being made by the medical profession.

19. For example, 029:00F; 055:31F, 083:54M; 096:33M; 099:26M.

20. For example, 229:29F, 203:20M.

21. For example, 197:19F.

22. For example, 230:26F; 157:28F; 244:28M; 232:19F.

23. Young persons, those under the age of eighteen years, but older than chil-

dren, can still be considered vulnerable persons. An athlete can be considered as more vulnerable if she or he is young or substantially younger (more than two years), same sex (in some conditions), of limited intelligence or with an impaired capacity to consent (Casswell 1996).

24. This is one of the few available figures regarding the occurrence of same-sex harassment, or of male to male harassment, in the Canadian sport context.

25. Naomi Levine, a lawyer, is the Sexual Harassment Officer at both the University of Winnipeg and Red River Community College.

26. Age is significant at the p.<.01 level and gender at the p.<.02 level.

27. Age is significant at the p. <.03 level and the stalker was always of the opposite sex (p. <.001).

28. Significance of the relationship was measured through chi-squared at p.<.02.

29. This is different information than that provided in the "forced sexual intercourse" question, and we have not yet checked whether there is overlap between the two questions. It may be that athletes see forced sexual assault and rape as different though, legally, they are the same experience.

Chapter Three

The Values of Sport:
The Other Side of the Medal[1]

At the trial of George William Smith, a track and field coach in Edmonton, Canada, one of the former club runners reports that when she was twelve years old, Smith "kissed her, rubbed her breasts and had her touch his penis on several occasions in his apartment" and another reports that she "had threesome sex with Smith and other female runners, at his encouragement" (Jimenez 1993a:B1). "50 year old Smith was sentenced to two and a half years for "two sexual assaults and one indecent assault" (Jimenez 1993b:A1).

On May 31, 1994, Gary Blair Walker, fifty years old and a convicted pedophile, was in court again, this time to see whether he would be declared a dangerous sexual offender. For over thirty years, he had been in numerous positions of trust with boys, including as a scout master, a hockey coach, a judo club manager and a church camp counsellor. In July of 1992, he had been convicted of thirty-five assaults against sixteen boys. In October 1992 he pleaded guilty to twenty-eight more charges. The *Toronto Star* reported that Walker had been convicted of sexual assaults on more than fifty boys and that "four of his victims, all from one

A24). Mr. Hanna, Mr. Roby and Mr. Stuckless are three men identified in a sex scandal involving the Maple Leaf Gardens facility employees or former employees. Gordon Stuckless had his prison sentence extended to five years from two years less a day in early May, 1999 and John Paul Roby, an usher at the Maple Leaf Gardens, was convicted on two counts of sexual assault, also in May 1999.

hockey team with which he was involved, took their own lives" (Mascoll 1994:A4).

What do these accounts have in common? First, they are taken from media stories about the conviction of individuals who have been coaches in the sport system. Unfortunately, most of what we know about sexual abuse in sport currently comes either from such media reports or from research done outside of the sport context and generalized to include sport. Second, both abusers are male, substantially older than the athletes they abused and were charged with multiple accounts of sexual assault. Smith assaulted only female athletes, one as young as twelve years of age. Walker assaulted only boys, about a hundred below the age of twelve and another hundred who were between twelve and fifteen (Mascoll 1994; A4). These profiles are similar to those of perpetrators of sexual assault outside the sport context. See for example the work of Elliott, Browne and Kilcoyne (1995). Third, both abusers used their position of trust and authority to gain sexual access to children and young persons. Fourth, the outcomes for the athletes were serious, ranging from experiencing years of psychological trauma to death.

These commonalities signal that sport has to be much more attentive about how it takes care of the participants in its charge. Children and young persons[2] participating in sport are not immune to such abuses and are in need of protection. They also show that those with sexual motives have access to children through their roles as leaders, in this case, as volunteer coaches, and that much more careful procedures need to be in place before allowing people to take on positions of authority and trust in sport. We believe that the starting place for efforts to eradicate such horrendous experiences is an evaluation of the way in which organized sport currently cares for its participants and the implementation of changes to ensure the safety of all participants.

As a strong advocate of the sport community's duty and obligation to respond to ethical challenges, the Canadian Centre for Ethics in Sport (CCES)is actively promoting ethical conduct in all aspects of sport globally. On the particular issue of sexual harassment and abuse in sport, the CCES sees sexual abuse as a betrayal of the "trust and loyalty that young people and their parents place in coaches and other guardians of our youth" (1997:1). Further, the CCES, along with the Canadian Association for the Advancement of Women in Sport (CAAWS),) has specifically acknowledged the gendered nature of sexual harassment and abuse in sport and has taken on such concerns as empowerment, abuse of power and the nature of a "perverted loyalty" that functions to keep athletes silent in the face of sexual abuse (1997:2).[3] We agree that sport needs just such leadership and stewardship to develop itself as a community which is responsible in responding to issues in sport which demand moral and ethical reasoning.

To more fully understand the dynamics within an "ethic of care" in the sport context, the terms trust and loyalty need some clarification. Trust can be defined as the believing in or relying on people, on what they say and on how they represent themselves to the world. Coaches and other persons in authority have what is called positional power and are accorded a measure of trust because of the positions they hold. Trust also means accepting the truth of a statement without evidence (*Concise Oxford Dictionary* 1983:601).

Loyalty is related to trust. Sport participants sometimes demonstrate their loyalty to sport and to those who facilitate their career development through trust. Some report feeling a love for sport and/or a duty to sport and express a strong and faithful allegiance to their sport and the sport world. This profound expression of loyalty is not to be underestimated in its power to ensure athletes become and remain hard working, committed, tenacious and relatively successful in the face of the many difficulties which arise.

One can sense a strong social network of relationships in which participants, particularly athletes, trusting of and loyal to those with authority over them, are groomed to achieve sporting success. In these relationships, the healthy interdependence of athletes and those in positions of authority over them is an essential ingredient for success. Yet, caution is necessary. It is in relationships such as these, we argue, where participants are also vulnerable to some of the sexual abuses which occur.

While sport enjoys an enviable reputation as an excellent environment for athletes to learn appropriate values for life, it is also fertile ground for violence, particularly sexual violence. As in other "touching professions," as Brackenridge (1996b) calls sport, mutual trust is essential to the building of appropriate coach-athlete relationships. In other words, sport organizations hold, or are given in trust, the responsibility for the full care of all participants while they are in the sporting context. This is called the "ethic of care," an ethic that ought to be at the very centre of sport.

The ethic of care can be summarized in three critical and interrelated points. The first is that sport organizations have a duty to exercise reasonable care in protecting participants from risk or harm and in offering them opportunity for quality experiences in sport. This can be called more specifically the duty of care, or the ethical, moral and legal obligations of an organization:

> ...the obligation of individuals or organizations to take reasonable measures to care for and to protect their clients to an appropriate level or standard. If the clients are vulnerable, if they cannot protect, defend, or assert themselves, permanently or temporarily, because of age, disability or circumstances, then that duty becomes more intense and the standard higher. (Street 1996:1)

The second part of an ethic of care is the assurance of fairness in sport practice, or what Loland and McNamee call a "mean of fairness" (1997:6). The fairness in sport must reach from the actual playing of the game out into all the other aspects of sport, including the social context within which all participate in the production and reproduction of sport. Loland and McNamee write that there is no room for what they call empty formalism—participants following identical rules or behaving in similar ways—in the search for the mean of fairness. Rather, the agreed upon rules and ethics must leave room for all participants to express themselves through sport according to their personal values and must allow diverse cultural and subcultural values to influence the development of sport (1997:6).

The third aspect of the ethic of care, and related closely to the second point, is that sport has an ethos, one that may be difficult to define but which is easily shared amongst sport participants. The ethos of sport is the character or spirit or belief system that underpins modern sport (Loland and McNamee 1997). It is made up of the people who live sport, the activities of sport, and even the work of sport. Sport exists only because we do sport. By doing sport, we create and recreate it as we go. Dedicated sport participants not only learn and follow formal rules but also experience, then embrace, a more comprehensive set of ethical principles. While it is clear that different athletes and different teams, even within the same sport, do not share identical views of the rules or have identical personal ethics, a shared sense of commonality within and through sport exists.

How then, we ask, is the duty of care discharged? Specific to the issue of sexual harassment and abuse in sport, the duty of care can be discharged by:

a) making a commitment to make sport better, thus taking into account the massive concern of the public about sexual abuse;

b) framing the debate in ethical terms, as more information and alle-

gations come forward;
c) reassuring the public that due diligence is in place and that progress is being made in reducing the incidences of such violence;
d) having the primary concern be the well-being, health and safety of the abused; and
e) providing support and assistance to those who have been harassed and abused.[4]

Unfortunately, it is clear that the leadership on challenges is not emerging from a great many organizations. Where leadership is evident is in the multi-sport organizations (e.g., WomenSport International, International Olympic Committee, Commonwealth Games Society) and in the clear thinking of the CCES approach, which shows a clarity of role and purpose and which also has the potential to take dramatic leadership on sexual harassment and abuse in sport.

THE CONTRADICTIONS: POWER AND THE POTENTIAL FOR VIOLENCE

Sport is, by and large, a wonderful experience for those who participate. Some claim that sport is one of the most significant and positive experiences of their lives. Given that sport has such an excellent reputation for fairness and that participation provides a good experience for both children and adults, how then can it also be the context within which violence, and in particular, sexual violence occurs?

It is our view that there are at least seven negative undercurrents in modern sport which may contaminate the experience for some participants. The undercurrents or political/cultural imperatives we have defined so far are patriotism/nationalism, militarism, competition, media sport, the work ethic, heterosexism/hypersexuality and familism.[5] When the negative aspects of these imperatives work alone or in concert, they encourage, facilitate and reinforce the poisoned stream of sport and in particular, the pollution of that stream by elements of discrimination and violence. While it may be difficult for some to accept the the existence of such forces , many sport participants are well aware of the negative undercurrents which taint sport. Our hope is that by identifying these imperatives, it will perhaps be possible to reduce or eliminate their effects.

We have grouped the seven imperatives into three loose categories. First are the imperatives related to development of a nation—patriotism/nationalism and militarism; second, are the imperatives related to upward mobility—competition, media sport and the work ethic; and third, are the imperatives related to sex, sexuality, eroticism and family—heterosexism/hypersexuality and familism.

Development of a Nation:
The Imperatives of Patriotism/Nationalism and Militarism

Sport and the development of nations and cultures are closely related. Both contain elements of a higher calling, one beyond the mundane realities of the everyday. For those in sport, patriotism/nationalism and militarism can be considered overlapping terms. The love for and devotion one feels to one's country is called patriotism and nationalism is the specific devotion one has to the well-being of a nation through support for its culture and collective interests. One's country and nation can be synonymous, though they are not always so. Militarism is an identification with the ideals of the professional military. Closely related, patriotism/nationalism and militarism are characteristics of sport participants' loyalty to their team and to the community or nation they represent.

Representative athletes, such as those travelling outside their community and wearing a team uniform, are expected to act correctly, to speak positively about their community or, in the case of national-team athletes, of their nation, and to be loyal to whom it is that they represent. Expectations are, for example, that Quebec athletes are loyal to the nation of Quebec; Aboriginal athletes to their First Nations or Peoples; and national-team athletes to Canada.[6] Such loyalty is reciprocated when the community or nation offers its fervent support to the team. In a sense, successful athletes are socialized to become ambassadors for their nation.

As organized sport has roots in the military preparation of young men for defence and war, it is not surprising that militarism is alive and well in modern sport. The need to ensure uniform appearance and disciplined behaviour, the unquestioned adherence of all to rules and regulations and the response to authoritative command are legacies of an earlier military tradition, which dominated the eighteenth- and nineteenth-century development of organized sport. Even the pomp and ceremony of modern multi-sport games is clearly based in military formations. Athletes marching in formation into a stadium, following the nation's flag and singing the national anthem have now become an expected part of the opening of the provincial/territorial or state games, the Olympic Games and others. Militarism goes even further. Sport participants are taught what behaviour is and is not acceptable. Reminiscent of battleground norms, athletes learn from coaches, co-competitors and the media about how to "toe the line," how to be "like the rest of the team" and to try to return to competition quickly, even after sometimes quite serious injuries (Kirby 1986). In the process, rules are clarified, regulations identified and penalties described. In this way, the traditional ways of "doing sport" are reinforced and replicated to such a degree that succeeding generations of teams have remarkably similar experiences and express themselves in comparable ways.

This is not to say that each sport or each community shares "fundamental value orientations" (Loland and McNamee 1997:6). We agree with Loland and McNamee that participants' commitment to a form of life or sporting practice does not necessarily ensure that values are shared, that homogenization occurs. It is true that, even within the same sport, two teams in a single locale can have very different norms and practices. One team could be characterized by its ability to use the rules and penalties to its advantage, another by its "nice players." Yet, we do want to make the point that conformity and uniformity within one's team or one's sport or to the ideals of one's nation or country are part of what athletes learn as they get increasingly successful in sport.

Loland and McNamee agree that there is some common ground based on shared values in sport and suggest those of fairness ("when voluntarily engaged in sport competitions, keep the shared ethos of the practice as long as the ethos does not violate basic, ethical principles and includes a sense of fairness") and play ("when voluntarily engaged in sport competitions, play to win") (1997:18). We would add that modern sport, particularly competitive, representative sport, is held within a social context in which the values found in patriotism/nationalism and militarism are actively inculcated in participants.

The imperatives of patriotism/nationalism and militarism are not always good for sport. Despite the importance of shared values and preparedness for competition, the imperatives are expressions of power, and as such, reinforce long-standing discriminatory attitudes and behaviours in sport. Characteristics, such as those of race, class, sex and language, enshrined as bases for discrimination in early sport, are reflected in the modern reincarnations of sport.

Modern sport has not yet committed to either completely integrated sport (homogeneity) or to separate but equal sport (heterogeneity) for the elimination of inequities (Lenskyj 1984). There are difficulties with both approaches. When the distinctiveness of particular groups of participants is lost, through, for instance, the building of "uniform" teams, with participants dressed to look alike and trained to act in like manner, homogeneity results. This ensures that distinctive group characteristics including race and ethnicity effectively disappear as part of the sport experience. Dorothy Strachan[7] suggests that the imperatives of patriotism/nationalism and militarism create a sort of cultural cleansing where sport teams appear both uniform and unified. By contrast, in the case of gender, the traditional discriminations and inequities continue to be perpetuated in modern sport practice. An excellent example of the distinctions based on traditional practice within sport is the rather unique view of "gendered patriotism" provided by Shona Thompson (1994). Thompson describes the Australian wives and mothers of crew members of a team leaving for a large international sailing race. The women stood on the docks, waving "their men" off to the competition in a way "reminiscent of the departure of troops for war zones." The women and children continue in the traditional role of spectators rather than as active participants in the upcoming competition.

Another aspect of the negative influence of patriotism/nationalism and militarism can be seen in local sport where loyalty to and pride for the team and its coach are part of a community's identity. In some cases, residents' identification with the participants can be so extreme that athletes become part of the community family and, as Brackenridge (1993) writes, the coach even becomes an athlete's surrogate family. Such local identification ensures two things: that civic boosterism and political conservatism become the hallmarks of the character of a well-adjusted athlete and also (and particularly negatively) that athletes' disclosures of problems of sexual harassment and abuse are very difficult to make. It is a "catch 22" situation for athletes experiencing sexual abuse because, on the one hand, they are bound by a code of loyalty and, on the other hand, they cannot easily "break the faith" or "break ranks" to reveal some of the more unsavoury aspects of their experience.

Athletes' difficulties in breaking ranks are seen in the 1997 case involving sexual assault charges against Canadian ice hockey coach Graham James. Both athletes who laid complaints testified that they had endured repeated sexual assaults over a number of years. Both had been afraid to make complaints because they feared losing their chance of playing in the professional NHL (National Hockey League). One of the two athletes laying charges chose not to have his identity revealed. The other, Sheldon Kennedy, revealed his identity to the public and has since been hailed as a hero for his courage.

Breaking ranks is difficult for other players too. Laura Robinson, in researching her book on sexual violence in ice hockey (1998), found numerous hockey players who would provide her with accounts off the record but all were very reluctant to go on the record with what they had seen, heard and experienced.[8] Despite the particular revelations in the Graham James case, the apparent sexual abuse problems in initiation rites and hazings (CBC 1996), the increase in the number of charges being laid against coaches and other sport figures, and the implementation of sexual harassment policies by many sport organizations, some individuals still suggest that the Graham James case is simply that of "an individual bad apple" in the coaching world[9] rather than symptomatic of a larger problem endemic to organized sport. The inability of individuals within sport organziations to offer healthy criticism of those organizations is one of the problems created by the fear of "breaking ranks."

Another issue within the patriotism/nationalism and militarism context is that of conflicting demands for an athletes' loyalty. Successful athletes may find themselves in the difficult position of concurrently representing more than one location or being named to more than one competitive team. While hometown coaches complain about national-team programs "taking the cream away from local programs," athletes are in another catch 22 situation, caught between their loyalty to the development coach and community and the chance to "make it big." To whom does an athlete owe her/his loyalty if named, for example, to a provincial team, a national junior team, and an all-star team at the same time? Whose demands take precedence? What sanctions arise when such conflicts occur?

A final issue closely related to the patriotism/nationalism and militarism imperatives occurs when some participants, usually those who are more successful and more conforming, are required to take on official ambassadorial roles for their teams, for example, participating in official functions and ceremonies, meeting dignitaries, representing their team for the receiving of awards and so on. Ambassadorial roles can be filled by coaches, athletes, administrators or anyone else involved in the official production of sport. Those who do not conform to the invisible standards set by the above imperatives are most unlikely to be granted the right to publicly represent their team. A more dangerous side of the ambassadorial requirements becomes evident when we look specifically at the situations of sexual harassment and abuse. First, the extra status, prestige and privilege accorded to ambassadors may serve as either a protection for individuals who are abusers or as a silencer for individuals who are victims. Second, individuals placed in ambassadorial roles may become isolated from the social supports they have as part of a team or group. As with most ambassadorial roles, sport participants have no real power. If they are already vulnerable, they can be made more vulnerable to abuse through separation from their social context.

The role of sport in the development of nations and of cultures provides sport with a wide range of impacts. Patriotism/nationalism and militarism, as imperatives, place enormous stress on sport participants to be "more than they are," to be representative of the best their community, their nation or their country can provide. While it is attractive on one hand to have the opportunity to represent one's nation or country, patriotism/nationalism and militarism also function concurrently to perpetuate the traditional and unequal power relations found in sport. This results in the sort of fertile ground in which discrimination and sexual harassment and abuse are known to occur.

UPWARD MOBILITY: THE IMPERATIVES OF COMPETITION, MEDIA SPORT AND THE WORK ETHIC

The imperatives of competition, media sport and the work ethic pressure individual participants to be upwardly mobile within the context of sport. This means that athletes work hard to reach their goals and to be the very best they can be. Aided by the ideologies of liberalism and individualism, participants seek to be fitter and stronger than ever before, to test themselves to the limit and to be successful within the carefully structured boundaries of organized sport. Sport participation is considered to be "both good and culturally superior" (Greaves, 1996:22) and participants come to expect status, prestige and reward for their successful endeavours.

The problem lies in the inordinate amount of emphasis on the individual. Individualism is "the belief in the primary importance of the individual and in the virtues of self-reliance and personal independence" (*Canadian Dictionary* 1996:693). When the onus is on individuals to train and perform within a competitive environment, the individual must go to great lengths to maintain her or his place in the "pecking order." Even the most successful competitors, coaches, administrators and officials know that as soon as their performances decline or they fall out of favour, they can be replaced. Rarely is sport a place where an individual can completely relax and enjoy participating, without the pressure of competition,.

Competition is not, in itself, good or bad. Competition takes a variety of forms including: against the self (setting a personal best performance, being the first international female referee), against other competitors (winning a match, being selected to be the team captain), against inanimate objects (climbing a mountain, passing a qualifying test as a coach), or against records (establishing a new world record, raising more money than last year). Competition can also occur "with" other players. Athletes have talked about coming up with their best performances when they have the best co-competitors or when they have the opportunity to "play up to the level" of a better team. The type of competition is specifically determined by the roots of each particular sport, and the great majority of sports depend upon a "competition against" rather than a "competition with" format.

One problem with competition lies in the gendered valuing of its outcomes. Sport competition generally occurs along gender lines, the assumption being that, unless gender is specifically mentioned, the competition involves male athletes. We have sport competition and women's sport competition. We have both the world record and the women's world record in the marathon. Universities have both a basketball team and a women's basketball team. Certain competitions are specifically for men, others specifically for women, some for both. And, although job specifications for positions in the coaching and administrative ranks are not nearly so explicit, overwhelmingly these are professions for males, and what is valued in a good candidate is of a gendered nature.

In the modern era, the Olympic movement has even tested athletes to ensure that those who compete in events for women are indeed female.

> Sport participants are not immune to the social pressures in society. Many Canadians at one time believed that sporting activity would effectively make women more manly, that is, sport participation would cast doubt on women's femininity. Still the femininity and often the heterosexuality of sportswomen is questioned. Gender verification testing still occurs in international competition to ensure that a) no men sneak into women's competitions and b) that no women with chromosomal abnormalities compete. Men do not undergo gender verification testing. (Kirby 1997a)

Although gender verification has been widely panned as essentially discriminatory and unscientific, has been abandoned by powerful international federations such as the International Amateur Athletic Federation (track and field), and is the subject of an aggressive lobby for its elimination, testing has continued at international competitions such as the Olympic Games. Progress has been made recently, with the abandonment of testing at the Pan American Games and at the Sydney Olympic Games 2000. However, this is seen as a temporary lull in testing while the International Olympic Committee gets the new code of ethics in place.

So, not only does sport reproduce the gendered nature of the social world, sport competition is one of the principle sites where gendered behaviour is learned and enforced. Some would even say that sport is where the "making of the male" occurs (Frank 1993), and statements like "she's as good as a man," "she throws like a man" and "the world record is ..." all rely on the use of a male norm. As long as sport competition remains organized principally along gender lines, the determination of success will continue to rely on a male norm, standard or record, and, in the case of women participants, will continue to be qualified by additional reference to performances of other females.

Through the existence of the competition imperative, sport remains an environment where boys and men are considered more successful than girls and women. Hence, males are accorded more power. And it is this gendered nature of power that is evident in sexual harassment and abuse. For instance, in our research, reported cases of sexual harassment and abuse in sport most often involve female participants who are harassed or abused by males. If a male sport participant believes that his maleness gives him superiority over female performers, he may also accept that he has the right to speak or act in a way which reflects his superiority. Thus, one of the ways to begin eliminating sexual harassment and abuse is to address the way in which males and females compete in sport and how their performances are valued. If the male norm continues to be used, an imbalance of power on the basis of gender remains, and the establishment of quality sport where individuals are respectful of each other's differences and similarities will not be possible.

The second imperative in this section involves the media creation of a "virtual reality of sport" for all concerned. In this, sport becomes larger than life—a place of heroism and legends, of terrible deaths and brilliant victories, and of records to be maintained and broken. Successful competition has come too often to mean "breaking the record" or of "doing what no one has ever done before." Of particular concern in this regard is the level of violence in sport. Both sport and the media have been much criticized for the level of violence which is produced in sport, and reproduced and perhaps exacerbated by the media for the public at large. The cultural polarities are clear: sport is a wholesome place for you and sport is a violent place where you have to learn to take care of yourself. The popularity in North America of "Rock'm Sock'm Hockey!" videos, of replays of fights in football and basketball games and of news items consisting of violent scenes from competitive sport are all testimony to duplicity of the media.

The media controls much of how the public and often those inside sport view issues of concern to sport participants. When sexual harassment and abuse occur, individuals in the media can work very hard to get information and have played a major role in raising the issue and educating athletes and the public about such occurrences.[10] However, the media can also be part of the problem. Media reporting tends to actually frame how the public and those in sport see the issues. If the media concentrates on the abuse of young male athletes, the public may not understand the enormity of the issue as it affects young female athletes. So too, the public nature of the media work can act to frighten athletes, coaches and even harassers/abusers away from dealing with such incidents. The media can play an important role in the eradication of sexual harassment and abuse but it is crucial that the framing of the sexual harassment and abuse issues be taken on by those within the sport domain.

Loosely interpreted, the work ethic, the third imperative in this section, means that those who participate in sport can expect success if they work hard and are very diligent. Rewards for their work come in a variety of forms. Some receive wages or salaries, prize money or bonuses. For others, rewards mean selection to representative delegations (national teams, international meetings) and involve the achievement of status and prestige. Sport organizations also benefit, through expanded mandates and budgets, better sport sites, improved popularity of their competitions and merchandise, and increased status of those working within the organizations. The difficulty with the work ethic imperative is that those who are unsuccessful are seen as not having worked hard enough. There is seldom a question of any responsibility by the sport organizations to address how that work might be structured and whether there are systemic problems which prevent certain individuals or groups from achieving. With the work ethic imperative, the onus remains on particular individuals to achieve within the established criteria.

The symbolic messages framing the work in sport include liberalism, individualism, glorification of the team (and within that, the performances of stellar individuals), "good" citizenship, health, maintenance of youth, heterosexuality and athleticism. Sport is reputed to be a good experience for all participants, and its "squeaky clean," healthy image can be used to sell products unrelated to sport.[11]

Work in sport is characterized by an uneasy balance between amateurism and professionalism, by voluntarism, career and the work ethic, quadrennial rotation of opportunities for competition, merit through competitive success, and sponsorship as a partial reward for success. Ann Peel of Athletes CAN (personal communication, August 1996) believes that, without an international association of athletes, competitors have little or no access to regulatory mechanisms of the workplace. The majority of amateur athletes are part of a volunteer workforce in a workplace where they have few rights and major performance responsibilities.

When all three imperatives (competition, media sport and the work ethic) work in concert, the result appears to be a heavy emphasis on the role of the individual in determining her or his experience and success within sport. However, in actuality, the ability of an individual to do so is heavily constrained by the structures of and conditions within which she or he works at sport. In general, upward mobility through sport is not available to all on an equal basis; nor is such mobility experienced in the same way by equally deserving participants. The opportunity to succeed is in reality determined by a system that has not yet come to grips with gender and other forms of discrimination and with problematic levels of violence.

SEX, SEXUALITY AND THE FAMILY: THE IMPERATIVES OF HETEROSEXISM/ HYPERSEXUALITY AND FAMILISM

Modern sport reflects, in its organization and functions, the patriarchal nuclear family model, including the appropriate norms and values. We base our discussion on three points, heterosexism (and its accompanying feature, compulsory heterosexuality, Rich 1980), hypersexuality (our own term), and familism (Bella 1992). We have come to understand that, not only is sport a gendered experience where participants learn "appropriate" gender roles, but that modern sport tolerates, even encourages the above forms of sexism. Together, these dominate sporting practice and work with other forms of discrimination to produce the chilly climate in sport, a climate where sexual harassment and abuse thrive.

Heterosexism is discrimination based on heterosexual privilege, where heterosexuality is seen as the social and sexual norm for all sport participants. It manifests itself through what Monique Wittig (1982:67) has called the "process of directing women into heterosexuality." This would apply equally to men. Like other forms of discrimination, heterosexism can be overt and covert.

In sport, the heterosexism can almost be regarded as an officially sanctioned discrimination. Sporting events are sexualised—sport is made glamorous but in a heterosexual way. For example, in figure skating pairs and ice dancing competition, where female and male athletes compete together, there is a ritualized heterosexuality displayed to the judges and the audience. The rules of the competition clearly distinguish between gender-appropriate performances for the female and the male. It seems that where judges are involved, athletes are trained to conform to and even exaggerate heterosexually appropriate behaviour. Even in events such as gymnastics, where female and male athletes do not compete together, the stylized performances portray ideal images of femininity and masculinity. Young, often pre-pubescent, girls perform routines in the gymnastics floor exercise that contain elements which some would call "soft" pornography. This glamour is both gendered and sexualised in a compulsorily heterosexual way, creating differing experiences of sport for female and male participants.

There are many ways for athletes to be glamourized in sport but it is the cultivation of the "feminine" and "masculine" which seems dominant. Organized sport tries to ensure "positive" (read heterosexual) images through careful orchestration of performance requirements and marketing. It is the androgynous woman or lesbian and the "not quite masculine enough" or gay man who provide obvious contradiction to the heterosexual imperative (Brackenridge 1993). For example, strategic marketing portrays successful male athletes (often with a pretty young woman on their arm), as masculine, heterosexual stars who are competitive and can be counted on when the going gets tough. Successful female athletes are often portrayed as "the girl next door" or with a boyfriend or husband, an assurance to the public of her heterosexuality.

In sport, the differences between males and females are pronounced and, any abuse which occurs does so within the context of males being more privileged than females. Some males may seek to prove their heterosexuality or their manliness through harassment of girls and women. As males are the most privileged, they are most often the harassers of females and less experienced males.

Brenda Richard (1996) writes that sexual harassment must be understood within the overall social context in which it flourishes. It is, for example, still acceptable for people to openly express anti-gay or anti-lesbian attitudes. Continued verbal, physical and sexual assaults (most unreported) are well known to gays and lesbians. Routine harassment and an oppressive climate in sport ensure that sexual contact is permitted only in heterosexual form. The message is that other forms of sexuality are abnormal and are unacceptable if participants want to be successful in sport. Heterosexism thus, reinforces sexism and is reinforced by homophobia. Gay and lesbian participants have a right to self expression through sport, though they currently lack the room to experience this right.[12] In value-based sport, homophobia and heterosexism would not be tolerated.

Hypersexuality is a gendered imperative that appears to be present in sport primarily for males. It is a phenomenon where the ideal image of a male athlete presumes also characteristics of great virility and super-active sexual (and heterosexual) appetite. There is abundant sex talk amongst many male athletes, talk filled with descriptions of whom they had sex with, how many times, and their sexual fantasies and plans (individually and collectively) for their next sexual conquest (CBC 1996). Hypersexuality is marked not only by the frequency of sexual activity but also by the apparent promiscuity and tendency to sexual violence of some athletes. Though the public may joke about the locker room talk of male participants, it is this talk which forms the overwhelming demand for athletes to be heterosexual and highly sexually active. Hypersexuality receives some official sanction and endorsement from the male sport culture through the organizational sponsorship[13] of initiation rituals filled with sexual hazing and danger for new players to a team.

Most of us would likely assume that a model coach would not be, nor would want to be, marked by the characteristics of hypersexuality as described above. Yet some coaches actively contribute to a sporting environment which is supportive of the hypersexuality of younger athletes. Such coaches provide personal stories of their own experiences, condone and sometimes participate in initiation and hazing rituals, and encourage sex-talk amongst male, and sometimes female, athletes. We see hypersexuality as the sexually-violent underbelly of a sporting culture which publicly promotes respect for colleagues and opponents and encourages safe and healthy living.[14]

We argue that, where heterosexism and hypersexuality exist, other discriminations, such as those based on race, age and able-bodiedness also flourish, and increase the potential for sexual harassment and abuse. The broad issues of racism, sexism, homophobia and heterosexism overlap and are part of the material reality of sexual harassment and abuse. In the human-rights context, harassment and abuse are specifically identified as forms of discrimination and hence, must be looked at as systemic and intentional problems.[15] Both kinds of discrimination, intentional and systemic, exist in sport. To improve our investigations of this problem, we must consider the intersectionality of sex and other forms of harassment (Samuels-Stewart 1996). In addition, we need culturally appropriate services which effectively remove obstacles and increase the options for the victims.[16]

When heterosexism and hypersexuality work together with the third imperative in this category, familism, the power dynamics of the patriarchal family are reproduced. Familism or the family imperative (Bella 1992) refers to the assumption of a hierarchical family structure, with a male "head of household," female (and heterosexual) spouse, plus children produced by the sexual union of the two adults. In this book we use the term familism to describe the way in which sport practice is organized along the same lines as a traditional nuclear family, with the athletes being provided with roles similar to those of children within a family structure (see Brackenridge 1993 for a description of this process for high performance athletes). Not only is such a family structure alive and well in sport practice, it is reproduced in organizations and in teams.

The family "unit" in sport consists of the team headed by the coach (usually male). To carry the analogy further, the close relatives who participate in some way in day-to-day family life are, in sport, the athletic trainers, sport physicians, sport psychologists, parents and siblings, and other personnel who contribute to an athletes' performances. At the national-team level, the training unit is also a patriarchal unit, one in which the head coach is virtually always male, and the role definitions and rituals for each family member (the team members) are carefully scripted along sport and gendered lines. An aura of "domesticity" is constructed to ensure athletes can meet all their social, emotional/intimacy and physical needs from within. Loyalty and self-sacrifice are encouraged. Problems within the family are not to be discussed outside; thus a context of secrecy about the dynamics of family relations is established.

Familism in sport provides fertile ground for a staggering amount of abuse of all kinds. Authority figures in sport appear to have ready access to athletes as sexual partners. The principles of loyalty and self-sacrifice ensure that athletes who experience sexual harassment or abuse will either internalize the problems or deal with them "in house." Sport will not be safe for athletes until the family imperative is challenged, and the practices of sport become more transparent.

The seven socio-cultural imperatives described above act in concert to not only form a dome of silence over sporting practice, but further to maintain and reinforce the very conditions in which sexual abuse thrives. Harassment and abuse compromise the otherwise respectful relationships which maintain quality sporting environments. We believe that quality sport can only be built by healthy participants, by those who are uncompromised by harassment and abuse. Further, if sport is to be seen as liberating for athletes,[17] then participants must have the freedom to compete fairly, equally and respectfully with others in an environment free of discrimination, harassment and abuse.

WHERE ARE WE NOW?

Some thirty years of research on sexual harassment and abuse exist, yet we are only now in a position to frame the issue of sexual abuse as it occurs in the sporting context. We, like Brackenridge (1997a), accept that within a continuum of sexual discrimination, sexual harassment and sexual abuse, it is possible to see the relationship between a sport environment tolerant of violence and sexism and the occurrence of sexual harassment and abuse.

Sexual discrimination exists in sport and contributes to what has been called a chilly climate for some participants (Joyce 1991:3). When participants, mostly girls and women, are actively excluded and undermined in sport, when their presence and contributions are regarded as unimportant, or when they face seemingly trivial incidents and behaviours which make them feel unwanted, they are experiencing the chilly climate. Both systemic and individual discrimination based on sexism, heterosexism and homophobia thrive within the chilly climate.

Sexual harassment refers to "the unwanted imposition of sexual requirements in the context of a relationship of unequal power. Central to the concept is the use of power derived from one social sphere to lever benefits or impose deprivations in another.... When one is sexual, the other material, the cumulative sanction is particularly potent" (MacKinnon 1979:1). Sexual harassment is further defined as unwanted attention of a sexual nature and includes:

- written or verbal abuse/threats,
- sexually oriented comments or jokes, or sexual innuendoes,
- taunts about body, dress, marital situation or sexuality,
- ridiculing of performance,
- sexual or homophobic graffiti,
- practical jokes based on threats,
- intimidating sexual remarks,
- propositions, invitations or familiarity,
- domination of meetings,
- domination of play space or equipment,
- condescending or patronizing behaviours which undermine self-respect or work performance,
- physical contact, fondling, pinching or kissing,
- vandalism on the basis of sex,
- offensive phone calls or photos, and
- stalking (*Ontario Human Rights Code* 1981, c. 53, s.6.).

Sexual abuse is an umbrella term for all forms of "sexually intrusive" behaviours and includes sexual touching, interference, exploitation and grooming, child pornography, prostitution and trafficking (Kelly et al. 1995). Sexual abuse is an abuse of power that occurs within the context of discrimination and "arises from a particular set of gender relations—dangerous relations—in which sexualities and sexual identities are shaped, maintained, challenged and resisted" (Brackenridge 1997a:10). Sexual abuse may include:

- groomed or coerced behaviours where there is an exchange of rewards and privileges for sexual favours,[18]
- assault committed in circumstances of a sexual nature using direct or indirect force, without their consent,[19]
- sexual interference with a child,[20]
- sexual touching,[21]
- sexual exploitation.[22]

There is much work yet to be done on the special case of consent. Consent is the voluntary agreement of participants to engage in the sexual activity in question. However, consent is not possible if one individual has a position of trust or authority over the other.[23] For sport, this point cannot be made strongly enough. The betrayal of athletes through sexual grooming by those they trust, particularly coaches and others in positions of authority, illustrates both the participants' vulnerability and the skill of the authority person as a manipulator. Further, in law, consent to sexual activity cannot be given by a child, someone with limited intelligence or impaired capacity to consent, a young person who cannot consent to what is being proposed, a person who is coerced, or a person who is unable to "be present" (e.g., is asleep).[24]

Sexual abusers are those who sexually abuse others. They may be persons in positions of authority or trust, persons in a relationship of dependency—e.g., coaches, administrators, referees, medical personnel and team selectors—other athletes, or they may be those who work in sport in a variety of volunteer and paid capacities. They may also be called harassers, molesters, sexual predators, rapists and pedophiles.

Although the practice of labelling sexual abusers by the various forms of abuse is somewhat controversial, we think it is important realize that sexual abusers appear as ordinary people in many ways. Some, like Kelly et al. (1995) argue that the labels we choose can allow us to disassociate sexual abusers from the other people in our lives. "By making them [sexual abusers] different from men we know [family and friends], the myth that most child abusers are strangers is maintained" (17). This labelling allows us to say, "These abusers are not like us" and paradoxically provides abusers with the perfect cover if they in fact do look like us. However, the way in which we refer to people must remain respectful. It is only when those suspected of sexual abuses are found guilty that they are sexual abusers or child sexual abusers.

Vulnerable participants are all those in sport—the novice participant, the high performance athlete, the coach, the manager, the sport medicine person, the ticket seller and so on—who may have difficulty protecting themselves from harm (Street 1996:1.6). However, some are likely to be more vulnerable that others. Children and young persons are more vulnerable than adults. Females are two to three times more likely to be sexually abused than males (Finkelhor 1979). What makes a person vulnerable in the sporting context is also related to the opportunity others have to influence or exploit them, particularly through a relationship of trust or dependence.

Sexual exploitation occurs when the sexual abuser establishes a relationship or uses an already established relationship, to gain sexual access to one or more of those who fall within the scope of his responsibility. Such activities have been called breaches of trust (Gonsiorek 1995) and in sport, depend on the ability of sexual abusers, sometimes called pedophiles or sexual predators, to groom vulnerable athletes (Brackenridge 1996a).

CONCLUSION: THE DOME OF SILENCE

In this chapter, we have described how organized sport is in conflict. It is caught between producing athletes competitive on the international stage and the terrible difficulties created by the dome of silence. We have also made the case that organized sport has both a duty and an obligation to respond to the challenges presented by the ongoing revelations about sexual abuse. Through our collaboration on this book, we have come to clearly understand how the seven imperatives (patriotism/nationalism, militarism, competition, media sport, the work ethic, heterosexism/hypersexuality and familism) dictate the shape and strength of the dome of silence.

The dome of silence has two functions. The first is to separate the public on the outside from the sport world on the inside. The second is to use the pressure created by the rarified atmosphere inside the dome to create a self-sufficient and self-perpetuating sport system which needs only a constant turnover of athletes committed to grasping the brass ring, an Olympic gold medal.

With the dome of silence in place, athletes should expect to find a "surrogate family" of coach-parent/friends and athlete-peer/friends. In their pursuit of competitive sport, they may find the best of support, the worst of abuse, or both, from such a family. Athletes who are sexually abused are most likely to find a wall of silence around them, where the person they would normally confide in is the abuser who exploited them, or the friend and associate of the abuser, and where their teammates are unsure about believing them. Within the dome of silence, athletes are unlikely to take action on behalf of their peers, fearing their own career jeopardy. Those outside the dome of silence rarely have anything to say about what happens to athletes inside organized sport.

The dome of silence protects those with sexual motives who grow up in or infiltrate organized sport. Like foxes in the hen house, sexual abusers who are also award winning coaches or others in positions of authority over athletes appear to have free rein in their actions. It is hugely problematic that current sport structures and the lack of safeguards mean that sport is a relatively safe place for sexual abusers. And, although great strides are being made, the dome of silence inhibits sport organizations from working alone or in concert to eradicate the abuse.

As Shona Thompson writes, "we need to watch carefully the ways in which dominant sporting ideologies and practices develop so that they do not become even more exploitative." (Thompson 1999:252). We believe there is a huge chasm between what sport should be doing and what it is doing. It is imperative that the dome of silence be eradicated from sport. The need for value-based sport and for the duty of care to be exercised by the stewards of sport is the key to better sport practice by all.

NOTES

1. Thanks are due to Celia Brackenridge and Mike McNamee of Cheltenham and Gloucester College of Higher Education, Cheltenham, U.K., and Victor Lachance at the Canadian Centre for Ethics in Sport for their helpful comments on this chapter.

2. Variations in the definition of a child or a young person influence, for example, definitions of sexual assault. In Canada, twelve years of age is the minimum age at which a person can be convicted "of an offence in respect of an act or omission on their part" (*Criminal Code*). A child is defined as under fourteen years of age; a young person is a person fourteen years of age or more but under eighteen years. With specific exceptions, the age of consent for sexual activity in Canada is fourteen years (*Criminal Code*, s. 13). The United Nations and the Council of Europe define childhood as those under eighteen and young adulthood as ages eighteen through twenty-one years (Kelly et al. 1995).

3. Such loyalty includes the team concept, that athletes will "walk through brick walls" for coaches, and the pressure some experience to maintain a silence (like the wall of silence around incest (National Film Board 1997)) when experiencing sexual abuse at the hands of someone in sport.

4. Information for points (d) and (e) provided by Victor Lachance, personal communication, June 12, 1997.

5. The bases of the analysis which produced the socio-cultural imperatives are from three sources: first, very fruitful discussions between the authors; second, from Greaves, who published *Smoke Screen: Women's Smoking and Social Control* (1996), which contains a comprehensive analysis of five socio-cultural imperatives for women who smoke (immorality, freedom, masculinity, heterosexuality, capitalism/patriotism); and third, from Shona Thompson (1994) of Murdoch University, who wrote about liberation, patriarchy, patriotism and capitalism in women's contribution to sport.

6. This was a bit awkward at the Francophonie Games in France in 1994 when Canada fielded three "national teams," Canada, Quebec and New Brunswick. Many of the athletes attending were unable to speak French.

7. Dorothy Strachan, personal communication, Ottawa, February 3, 1997. Strachan suggests that coaches with considerable power may even enable athletes to "become something they are not" or to take on the role of ostracizing each other to increase the degree of athlete uniformity and "fit."

8. Personal communications with Laura Robinson between March and June 1997.

9. Several callers on radio open-line talk shows Kirby did with the CBC in Saskatchewan and Edmonton in January 1997 held this view.

10. Journalists such as Alison Smith and James Christie (*Globe and Mail*), Mary Hines and Robin Brown (CBC Radio), John Brown (*St. John's Telegraph*), Wendy Long (*Vancouver Province*), Alan Adams (*Ottawa Citizen*) and Lori Ewing (*Calgary Herald*) have contributed much to raising public awareness of the issue. However, three television programs in 1993 first captured the Canadian public's attention: an April transmission of *The Shirley Show*, a talk show which featured retired high performance athletes in disguise, the July 8th CBC *Primetime* on sexual harassment, and the November

2, edition of *The Fifth Estate*, an internationally respected investigative journalism program with Hana Gartner. In late 1996 and early 1997, the Graham James case initiated another media storm for authors Kirby and Greaves. In all, they have done well over one hundred interviews in various media since July 1996 when the statistical data presented in Chapter Two of this book were first reported. This included interviews with the majority of Canada's and some major U.S. newspapers; interviews and/or call-in programs with numerous radio stations; interviews with CBC (*Newsworld*, *McLeans Hour*), CTV (*Canada AM*), RDI (*Nouvelles*), BBS national TV (the Dini Petty and Camilla Scott talk shows); and magazines such as *Macleans* and the *Christian Science Monitor*.

11. Recently, testimonial advertisements by Canada's Olympic athletes have capitalized on the athletes' good character, success as national-team athletes and Olympic medal winners and the public's recognition of them as stars to sell beauty products.

12. Gays and lesbians in sport have little social purchase. The promotion of the gay/lesbian lifestyle in sport is invisible except through the international development of the Gay Games. Further, there is the continued strength of the myth that "being in the closet" is about choice. Richard (1996) reminds us that it is an unenviable place to be. Richard also reminds us that homophobic stereotypes used to amuse heterosexuals leave gays and lesbians open to ridicule.

13. Most sport organizations would not admit openly their support of hazing or initiation rituals, even when such events do not involve sexual danger. Yet, the pervasiveness and durability of these rituals involving sexism and sexual activity across a variety of sports suggest that because they touch at the very heart of sport tradition and will therefore be difficult to eradicate in some sports.

14. Together, heterosexism and hypersexuality explain why, though Magic Johnson is a tragic figure for AIDS workers, his hero status as an athlete was confirmed when it was revealed that he's had sex with numerous women. He "fulfiled every man's sexual fantasy" and took a place in history as one of the great male sport superstars!

15. In addressing the values of sport, it is important to understand that an absence of justice and freedom are part of the experience of sexual exploitation. The 1989 United Nations Convention on the Rights of the Child contains the following:
    • freedom of expression, of thought and conscience,
    • freedom from abuse and neglect, and
    • freedom from discrimination.

16. Krause (1996) says that violence is not accepted in any country although there may be tacit support for it. It is important that we, in Canada, challenge the norms of behaviour which are sexist and don't excuse the harassment or abuse, but realign it. There is, Krause says, a need for culturally appropriate services.

17. Sport is also liberating for boys and men but we would argue that sport experience for girls and women is unique and distinct from that of males. The liberation itself has a gendered character. And when liberation is con-

strained, it is experienced differently by females and males. Thus, if sport is a gendered experience conducted within a sexist society, when sexual harassment occurs, it is experienced differently by males and females. Girls and women are not as secure in sport as males, participating somewhat as visitors in something designed by and for men. Harassment threatens the very participation of all girls and women and is the fine edge of misogyny.

18. "Assault causing bodily harm—any hurt or injury to a person that interferes with the health or comfort of the person and is more than merely transient or trifling in nature" (*Criminal Code*, supra footnote 1, section 267 (2). Aggravated assault causing bodily harm—"wounds, maims, disfigures or endangers the life of the complainant" (*Criminal Code*, supra footnote 1, section 268).

19. Section 256(1) of the *Criminal Code*.

20. Section 151 of the *Criminal Code* provides that a person who, for a sexual purpose, touches directly or indirectly, with a part of the body or with an object, any part of the body of a person under the age of fourteen years, commits an offence.

21. Section 152 of the *Criminal Code* provides that a person who, for a sexual purpose, invites, counsels or incites a person under the age of fourteen years to touch, directly or indirectly, with a part of the body or with an object, the body of any person, including the body of the person who invites, counsels, or incites and the body of the person under fourteen years, commits an offence. Note: consent is not a defence unless the accused is less than two years older than the complainant and neither is in a position of authority towards the complainant nor a person with whom the complainant is in a relationship of dependency (*Criminal Code*, supra footnote 1, sections 150.1(1) and 150.1(2)).

22. Sexual Exploitation of a Young Person, section 153(1) (a) of the *Criminal Code*, provides that "a person who is in a position of trust or authority toward a young person or is a person with whom the young person is in a relationship of dependency and who for a sexual purpose, touches, directly or indirectly, with a part of the body or with an object, any part of the body of a young person, commits an offence." Section 153(1) (b) provides that "a person who is in a position of trust or authority toward a young person or is a person with whom the young person has a relationship of dependency and who for a sexual purpose, invites, counsels, or incites the young person to touch, directly or indirectly, with a part of the body or an object, the body of any person, including the body of the person who so invites, counsels, or incites the young person to touch." Sexual exploitation also includes boundary violations and betrayals of trust of a sexual nature.

23. The person's consent does not afford the accused a defence on a charge of sexual exploitation of a young person under section 153 (young persons fourteen to seventeen inclusive) where the accused is charged with an offence under section 151 (sexual interference with a child) or section 152 (invitation to a child to sexual touching), 160(3) (bestiality in the presence of a child or inciting a child to consent to bestiality) or section 173(2) (exposing genitals to a child for a sexual purpose) or is charged with an of-

fence under section 271, 272, or 273 (sexual assault provisions, in respect of a complainant under the age of fourteen years, it is not a defence that the complainant consented to the activity that forms the subject matter of the charge." (Casswell 1996:99) Also see R. v. M. (L.A.), supra footnote 21, at 185 (Man.R.), per Clearwater J.

24. Consent would also be vitiated if the agreement is expressed by words or conduct of someone other than the complainant; the complainant is incapable of consenting; the accused induces the complainant to engage in the activity of abusing a trust, power, authority; the complainant expresses a lack of agreement to engage in the activity; the complainant, having consented to engage in sexual activity, expresses a lack of agreement to continue to engage in the activity.

Chapter Four

Coach-Athlete Relations:
An Alternative Ethical Framework

INTRODUCTION

While sexual harassment and abuse have been well-documented as serious social problems for all of society, the sporting world is particularly vulnerable to such abuses because it is an environment characterized by close relationships ("Stopping Sexual Abuse in Sport" 1997). More often than not, such close relationships are between athlete and coach.[1] These relationships are not unlike other relationships of trust, dependency and authority which exist between physicians/therapists and patients, teachers and students, and clergy and members of their congregation. In close relationships of dependency and trust, there are special vulnerabilities to harm and exploitation. As McNamee (1998:158) points out, "situations in which coaches find themselves can introduce temptation into human relationships." Mostly, coaches behave responsibly, respectfully and ethically, working with athletes to make the best possible decisions. However, occasionally, coaches abuse their power and use sport to better themselves or to meet their own needs ahead of those of the athletes. The misuse of power includes sexual harassment and abuse of athletes. In response, the sporting world is confronted with acknowledging such harassment and abuse and is struggling to develop adequate responses in the forms of prevention and intervention.

In this chapter we explore the dynamics of the coach-athlete relationship. We also review and assess responses by the Canadian sporting world to sexual harassment and abuse. The argument that we develop builds upon a position first discussed by M.J. McNamee (1998)—that, while it is imperative to have rules, protocols and ethics of conduct to guide coach-athlete relations, there are limitations to what we can expect of such measures. By themselves, they may not be adequate for making the kinds of substantive changes to coach-athlete relationships or to the values of the sporting world that would ensure the security of athletes. Admittedly, the Canadian sporting world has moved to identify the values which should underpin sport, the most important being that sport be "athlete-centred." What is absent from the discourse surrounding athlete-centred sport is a serious analysis of the kinds of fundamental ethical shifts which need to occur to realize such a goal.

We propose an alternative ethical framework—an ethic of care—to help guide coach-athlete relations and, more importantly, to inform the transformation of the general sporting culture in which such relations operate.

THE COACH-ATHLETE RELATIONSHIP

The athlete is "any individual who engages in sport, at any level, within the context of amateur sport. Athletes are (or ought to be) the raison d'etre of the sport system ... and in order to maintain the integrity and value of sport, it is critical that the sport experience be positive for athletes" (Canadian Heritage 1994:17). Traditionally, however, athletes have been amongst the very last to be considered when decisions have been made which directly affect them. Moreover, coaches have held and continue to hold a lot of power over athletes. Coaches spend a significant amount of time with their athletes, and "coaches of elite children's sports, by spending the bulk of every day with their athletes, can influence these children more than their parents or their teachers at school" (Joan Ryan as quoted in "Sex, Lies and Volleyball" 1996:81). Indeed as Tomlinson and Strachan (1996:iii) point out, "The intimate nature of sport gives coaches entry into athletes' lives outside the traditions, social structures, and conventions that come with being a family member, a longtime friend, or community member." One might argue that the coach-athlete relationship is akin to a personal relationship. Coaches therefore have a number of different types of power including: positional power, personal power, reward power, coercive power, expert power, information power, resource power, relationship power and enabling power (Werthner 1995:8). Coaches and other persons in authority are accorded a measure of trust because of the positions they hold and often proceed with their day-to-day duties and obligations without experiencing any scrutiny or supervision.

The relationship between coach and player is inherently unbalanced, and the potential for an abuse of power or authority is great. In particular, as examples from our study (some of which were also related in earlier chapters) illustrate, abuse of power can result in many forms of sexual harassment and abuse:

> A much older coach [fifty-three] became sexually involved with a young [seventeen-year-old] athlete and manipulated her into an act of defiance against her former coach, sport governing body and eventually her family. She left home to live with him in a foreign country and had not contacted them in over a year. I don't know if this qualifies as abuse or harassment but I think it's still an exploitation of power and probably significant.

One of my teammates slept with the coach [forty-three] since she was thirteen. She felt awful because she couldn't say anything to anybody. The sexual abuse happened on team trips, in his trailer, in his vehicle, in the hotel and in many other places. The coach said how special she was and he took her on as his special project. He coached her as his special project, so special that he slept with her until she was eighteen. He completely isolated her from the rest of us. (200:36F)

The situation was harassment and it was by a friend in a position of power, my coach. The use of the position was not even recognized by him. The abuse happened in his home. It's difficult to describe. It was more of an ongoing situation where coach/athlete/friend was beginning to get confusing—when were you just a friend or athlete or coach? When you work closely with someone for so long, it [the relationship] gets taken for granted and people feel they can say or do anything they want. (120 28F)

Coaches using their authority to take advantage of students, one during regular training and at his home. A long-time coach with a close and trusting relationship with the student began inviting her to his home for "extra" training-related sessions. He subtly began to sexually harass/molest her in such a way that she was afraid to speak up about the issue for a long period of time. (064:19F)

When the coach sleeps around with his athletes in an ongoing [way, the coach is] in my mind, preying on them from a position of trust, despite the fact that both the coach and the athletes would likely claim that the sex was consensual. (157:28F)

When there is an abuse of power—such as sexual harassment or sexual abuse—the institution of sport is damaged, and the entire coaching profession is undermined. Most importantly, the athlete is harmed. And as Marilyn Friedman has argued:"when someone is harmed in a personal relationship, she is owed rectification of some sort, a righting of the wrong which has been done her. The notion of justice emerges as a relevant moral notion" (1993:265). Accordingly, the sporting community has drawn upon legal guidelines, policies, protocols and codes of ethics in an attempt to both prevent and respond to harms such as harassment and abuse in a just manner.

LEGAL GUIDELINES

Using Canada as a case study, it is possible to see how one country's justice system has responded to the problem of sexual abuse by establishing legal requirements for consent. Moreover, legal precedent has also been set regarding the illegality of a person in trust having any sexual contact with individuals over whom they exercise power.[2]

For example, according to the 1990 Department of Justice Canada's *Law on Child Sexual Abuse: A Handbook:*

- Sexual activity without consent is always a crime regardless of the age of the individuals.
- Children under twelve are never considered able to consent to sexual activity.
- Children twelve or more, but under fourteen, are deemed unable to consent to sexual acts except under specific circumstances involving sexual activity with their peers.
- Young persons fourteen or more but under eighteen are protected from sexual exploitation, and their consent is not valid if the person touching them for a sexual purpose is in a position of trust or authority over them or if they are in a relationship of dependency with that person.

True consent cannot be obtained if the relationship with the person is one of trust or authority such as between athlete and coach. As Hilary Findlay of the Centre for Sport in Law in Ottawa explains: "[Trust and authority] are the very essence of the coach/athlete relationship" (as quoted in "Coaching, Trust and Sex" 1997:5).

INSTITUTIONAL RESPONSES

In many ways, although authorities in sport across Canada have been aware for a long time of the problem of coaches harassing young athletes (Rinehart 1996), sport has been behind many other societal institutions and organizations in dealing with and responding effectively to sexual harassment and abuse. However, in the wake of recent public revelations of sexual abuse of athletes, most professional organizations have developed detailed policies and/or codes of ethics which demonstrate an intolerance for sexual harassment and abuse. Such policies guide the behaviour of individuals who hold positions of power and trust by detailing their rights, obligations and duties to those over whom they have authority.[3] Such measures are intended to create organizational climates more conducive to reporting sexual harassment and abuse and, at the same time, to preventing their occurrence. With such provisions, the sporting community hopes to re-establish itself as a posi-

"Long history of sex-abuse complaints in swimming"—the cases of Derry O'Rourke and George Gibney (from *The Irish Times on the Web*, Sat., Jan. 31, 1998).

Johnny Watterson, who has been investigating sex abuse in Irish swimming for four years, comments on the O'Rourke case and related problems facing sport:

The mother was horrified. What her young teenage daughter had told her has become a modern parental nightmare. Her swimming coach had sexually assaulted her. It started with what might be termed a grope: the coach wanted to measure her pectoral muscles. But it didn't stop there.

It was late 1992. The club was connected to a Dublin secondary school. The horrified mother wrote a letter of alarmed complaint to the club. Following an investigation the club told her there was no foundation for her daughter's complaints. The mother accepted the club's assurances.

But almost a year later the headmaster of the school where the club swimming pool was situated dispatched a missive to the coach, Derry O'Rourke.

"I have been made aware of certain complaints about your behaviour in the pool/changing room area in the past. Investigations are in progress. If these investigations prove to be of a serious nature, there could be serious consequences for the school. Pending the outcome of these investigations, it is my duty to tell you that you are suspended from work on full pay until further notice. You are not to enter the school premises as coach, lifeguard or parent until further notice from me."

A week later the secretary of the swimming club wrote to Garda Commissioner Patrick Culligan stating the situation surrounding O'Rourke. The letter stated: "There was only one instance in the past 22 years of coaching to this committee's knowledge of a complaint by a family regarding their daughter which might have been construed as sexual, which was investigated by three committee members, who gave unanimous agreement that the complaint was mistaken and the incident without foundation."

Last December Derry O'Rourke pleaded guilty to sexually assaulting the young girl whose complaint had been investigated by the three committee members and discovered to be without foundation.

Sadly for some children who joined swimming clubs for fun and healthy exercise, Derry O'Rourke was not the only poolside pedophile stalking youngsters. In swimming circles, the case of another highly respected coach is now an eight-year-long scandal. It concerns George Gibney who, like O'Rourke, scaled the heights and coached the Irish Olympic team.

In December 1990 another coach was contacted by a swimmer trained by Gibney. The swimmer told the coach that Gibney had abused him. The coach decided to act and "approached an IASA [Irish Amateur Swimming Association, the sport's controlling body] executive member at the pool.

"I said I wanted advice and explained that I had heard a number of allegations concerning George. 'I know where you heard them... [the victim was named],' said the official ... A short time later I requested a meeting with Frank McCann as president of the Leinster branch."

"I met him outside the Aisling Hotel in Dublin. I had also heard rumours of other things, and had personal experience of a swimmer suffering from an eating disorder and who was threatening to take her life."

"He said that he 'hoped to f... that it did not break while he was president.' He said that I could do nothing and neither could he. He also said I should back off and leave it alone."

The young swimmer the coach was talking about subsequently made a number of unsuccessful attempts to take her life. She was one of Gibney's victims. Last August, McCann was convicted and jailed for murdering his wife and 18-month-old niece.

However, once the school where Gibney held his swimming lessons became aware of the allegations again him, they suspended him, in marked contrast to the attitude of the swimming association. In a furious letter to the IASA, one parent, Aidan O'Toole, father of Irish European silver medallist Gary O'Toole, gave an indication of parental feelings.

"Within the last 14 days," Mr O'Toole wrote in July 1993, "Mr Gibney has been charged with 27 offences. I would also like to remind you that Mr Gibney was in charge of a course held in Newpark [school] last December organized by the Leinster branch of the IASA. At this stage some the officers knew about the pending charges."

The case against Gibney was discontinued. But he was later exposed when his victims, in sworn affidavits, told their stories in the *Sunday Tribune*. Gibney did not sue: he fled the country.

Not once has the IASA issued a statement in support of abuse victims of swimming coaches. None has beet contacted by the IASA to verify the authenticity of their claims. Not one official apology has been received by any of the children who alleged that Gibney abused them. No internal investigation has been initiated by the IASA substantiate the claims. No significant change in procedure has taken place to ensure that children are protected in the sport. No effort has been made to provide counselling of victims who might need it—and many do.

No impact study has been initiated despite the fact that majority of the approximately 6,000 members of the IASA are children.

Yesterday the Minister for Sport, Dr McDaid, told the Irish Amateur Swimming Association that he wanted to meet them ... urgently and at the earliest possible date.

Last year the taxpayer, via the Government, gave the IASA £230,000.

tive, accountable institution deserving of public support and trust.

For instance, in September 1996, Sport Canada said that, as a prerequisite to receiving federal monies, national sport organizations would be required to put anti-harassment measures in place. In reaction, Canadian sporting organizations have developed a wide range of policies, rules, regulations. It is important to note, however, that the development of such responses has been reactive and uneven. These policies are largely driven by the need to avoid liability and increase public accountability. For the most part, their limitations are not adequately understood. Specifically, there is too much reliance on these policies alone to make a transformative impact on the cultural context of sport.

Many organizations who have established these "stand-alone" policies have followed the Law Society of Upper Canada 1992 publication, *A Recommended Personnel Policy Regarding Employment-Related Sexual Harassment*, and the 1994 guidelines, *Harassment in Sport: A Guide to Policies, Procedures and Resources*, published by the Canadian Association for the Advancement of Women in Sport and Physical Activity. The latter recommends that every harassment policy contain the following:

- a policy statement declaring that the sport organization is committed to providing a work and sport environment free from harassment and that harassment will not be tolerated;
- a statement setting out what persons and what situations are covered by the policy;
- a definition of harassment along with examples of the types

of behaviour which constitute harassment;
- an effective, understandable and manageable internal complaint mechanism which fairly balances the rights of both the complainant (the person making the complaint) and the respondent (the person against whom the complain is made); (The mechanism should include options for informal resolution of complaints, mediation of complaints, and where these fail or are inappropriate, formal investigation of complaints.)
- a declaration of the sport organization's commitment to take appropriate disciplinary action whenever a complaint of harassment is substantiated; (The policy should specify what types of discipline are appropriate for what types of infractions.)
- a parallel provision for taking disciplinary action against those who bring false, vexatious, or frivolous charges of harassment;
- assurances of confidentiality to both complainant and respondent;
- provisions to protect the complainant from retaliation or reprisal; and
- an appeal mechanism available to both the complainant and the respondent.

In 1998, this information was augmented with a website and guide developed by the Harassment and Abuse in Sport Collective[4] for sport clubs and associations to assist them in dealing with harassment and abuse. The vision of the collective is:

... that there shall be no abuse, neglect and/or harassment, whether physical, emotional or sexual, of any participant in any of its programs. Every parent, volunteer and staff member should take all reasonable steps to safeguard the welfare of participants and protect them from any form of maltreatment. (1997:website)

Their guide entitled *Speak Out! ... Act Now!* provides detailed information on how organizations and individuals can work towards preventing and responding effectively to harassment and abuse. This includes guidelines for developing policies and procedures and for responding to harassment complaints and abuse disclosures as well as information on legal remedies and the duty to report.

In addition to the implementing policies and protocols, national sporting organizations have been developing education and training workshops for their athletes, coaches,[5] administrative personnel, and medical staff regarding these provisions. Athletes Canada has organized two national workshops on harassment in athletics. Many organizations, such as Ringette Canada, Canadian Fencing Federalism, and the Canadian Paralymic Committee, have appointed harassment officers. In 1996, the Canadian Association for the Advancement of Women and Sport and the Canadian Amateur Diving Association sponsored a harassment complaint investigation skills training workshop for harassment officers in sport organizations. And some, like the Canadian Figure Skating Association include the role and responsibilities of a harassment committee in their membership harassment policy.

Generally speaking, most Canadian sporting organizations' harassment policies apply to all employees as well as to all directors, officers, parents, volunteers, coaches, athletes and officials. Only a few, such as Biathlon Canada, Gymnastics Canada, Judo Canada, Softball Canada, Water Polo Canada, Football Canada, Canadian Fencing, Ringette Canada, Canadian Paralympic Committee and Canada Games Council, have specific sections in their harassment policies addressing coach-athlete sexual relationships. The following example fron Judo Canada illustrates the way these policy statements are generally worded:

> Judo Canada takes the view that intimate sexual relationships between coaches and adult athletes, while not against the law, can have harmful effects on the individual athlete involved, on other athletes and coaches and on Judo Canada's public image. Judo Canada therefore takes the position that such relationships are unacceptable for coaches coaching at the National Team level. Should a sexual relationship develop between athlete and coach, Judo Canada will investigate and take action, which could include reassignment, or if this is not feasible, a request for resignation, or dismissal from employment. (1997: 54)

Some policies include unique responses to harassment and abuse. For example, the Canadian Freestyle Ski Association includes in its 1993 harassment policy a section entitled, "What to do in a Sexual Harassment Emergency." While this particular example could use more information and refinement in its explanations, having a practical, step-by-step guide to responding to sexual harassment is a useful tool to include in any harassment policy.

Law, policy rules and regulations are necessary responses to sexual harassment in the sport context as they are intended to preserve proper human relationships in professional situations (McNamee 1997a: 6). Policies regarding sexual harassment and abuse in sport are also necessary for setting out certain moral minimums (duties, obligations, principles and rules)[6] so that individuals refrain from harming others. In this way, the policies can serve as a map or guide for members of sport organizations. They also fill the self-expressed need of athletes. As one respondent to our survey notes:

> It needs to be clear where the coach/athlete relationship stands. When you work with someone 24 hours per day, 6 days a week for 6 years, it develops into a friendship—so when/if the coach sleeps with another athlete—there needs to be a clear code of conduct for coaches.

These policies also clearly establish that sport organizations and their members have a responsibility for preventing harassment or abuse and, moreover, that there are penalties for those persons in authority who do not act accordingly.

And yet, policies and codes of conduct or even codes of ethics, which are more detailed, are in and of themselves inadequate for ensuring ethical behaviour. Similarly McNamee has argued:

> Codes of conduct may indeed be indispensable to the safety-net task of catching those who are unprofessional in their conduct and enabling their punishment and/or expulsion. What they cannot do, and what they should not be expected to do, is to have any great effect in ensuring ethical behaviour per se. (McNamee 1998:167)

This is because ethics and ethical conduct cannot be simply reduced to the idea of rule responsibility. As McNamee (1998) also points out, there is no rule book that can describe or predict all possible actions that may be considered unprofessional. Policies and codes of conduct after all are subject to interpretation, negotiation and conflict. The limitations of sexual harassment policies is alluded to by one of our respondents in the following:

> I think many NSOs have some form of sexual harassment policy in sport to some degree. However, it is my opinion that this policy needs to be addressed to the athletes, administration and coaches so that there is a "clear" picture of what types of actions or conducts are acceptable, unacceptable, etc. (112:23M)

In order to promote ethical behaviour and the highest ideals of conduct, discourse needs to move beyond a focus on how moral behaviour consists in the avoidance of wrong acts (McNamee 1998:154) to include a discussion of values. A much more fundamental or radical approach is needed, one that really makes us evaluate how sport as an institution can reduce and ultimately eliminate the sexism which it currently reproduces in the form of sexual harassment and abuse. For such a transformation to occur, a change in attitude, which comes from examining the broader social context, must accompany changes in rules and policies.

Accordingly, we propose the investigation of a set of values and moral assumptions that could inspire actions and responsibilities which transcend the minimums necessitated by rules and regulations. Sport requires a comprehensive and clear ethical framework in which to contextualize its rules, regulations and codes of ethics. It needs a theoretical foundation that can unite and morally guide the entire sporting community.

MORALITY, VALUES, ETHICS AND SPORT

Morality is involved with values and principles to which reference can be made before making a decision or engaging upon a particular course of action (Arnold 1997:86). A definite relationship exists between sport and morality. Like the practices of medicine or engineering, it is a part of the social fabric of community life (Arnold 1997:68), and therefore subject to moral prescriptions and precepts. Although traditionally, sport has been seen as "morally good" (Brackenridge 1994), with the increasing awareness of drug abuse, harassment, and physical and sexual abuse, the moral goodness of sport has been challenged.

Since the initiation of the Dubin Inquiry in 1988,[7] Canadian sport has attempted to articulate the values which should underlie the Canadian sport system. Values can be understood as "deeply held ideas of what is desirable, something worth having or believing" (Tomlinson and Strachan 1997:67). Attempts to articulate sporting values can be found in *A Planning Framework for Sport in Canada*, which was developed to provide a sense of unity and purpose as well as "co-ordination and focus for the activities of the key agencies providing leadership to Canadian sport" (Canadian Heritage 1994:4). This document defines a set of underlying values for the sport context:

> All partners and stakeholders involved in the Canadian Sport System promote and strengthen the values associated with sport, including:
> • sport is valued in and of itself;
> • sport is accessible for all Canadians;
> • opportunities exist for all Canadians to progress from recreational to high performance sport according to personal inter-

est, aspirations, and abilities;
- sport is based on and reflects positive values and ethics including achievement, enjoyment, responsibility, safety, teamwork, respect, and fair play;
- sport includes the pursuit of excellence and the desire to win within a fair and ethical environment and that ... sport contributes to the physical, moral, and social development of Canadians. (Canadian Heritage 1994:4)

Note that positive values and ethics are highlighted and include responsibility and safety, competition in a fair and safe environment and that sport should contribute to the physical, moral and social development of Canadians. Presumably, if these were fully realized within sport, the opportunity for and toleration of sexual harassment or abuse would cease to exist. However, at this time, some athletes still find themselves competing in unsafe environments with unsafe people, some of whom would not endorse these sport values. The goal of achieving value-driven sport is a difficult but important one. With that achievement, all participants in the sport community, from the athletes to the fans, would be able to fully and unreservedly promote and strengthen these values through their association with sport.

It is interesting to note that, even before the revelations of sexual abuse in sport exploded in the media in 1993 with the CBC television program, *The Fifth Estate*,[8] those in sport were already struggling to provide the very best care for athletes in their trust. Through much consultation and with the endorsement of sport (as represented by the Canadian Sport Council) and of governments, critical themes were identified for the purposes of guiding sport. Identified themes, listed below, received provincial, territorial and federal ministerial approval in March 1993 and published in the above mentioned report, *A Planning Framework for Sport in Canada*, in 1994:

- athlete-centred system,
- leadership,
- values and ethics,
- equity and access,
- sport development,
- pursuit of high performance athletic excellence,
- public interest in sport.

It was anticipated that these themes would give the sport community a "sense of shared accomplishment as [they were] achieved" (Canadian Heritage 1994:5) Two discussion papers appended to that report, one on equity and access and the other on athlete-centred sport, contain early identification of the problem of harassment in sport. Parts of the discussion papers are highlighted here because they are instructive in the values they prescribe for Canadian sport and are useful for understanding how institutionalized sport frames the harassment issue.

EQUITY AND EQUITABLE ACCESS

Equity and equitable access are important values against which the culture of sport can measure itself and, to measure well, equity and access must be evident in the day-to-day practice of sport. Organizations such as the Canadian Association for the Advancement of Women in Sport (CAAWS), Sport Ontario, the Commonwealth Games Association of Canada (CGAC), the Canadian Intercollegiate Athletic Union (CIAU) and Promotion Plus (B.C.) have already demonstrated that they are part of the committed leadership which is key to changing sport (Canadian Heritage 1994:36). They see that the task for Canadian sport is to bring all sport organizations (local, regional and national) and all individuals participating in any aspect of sport to endorse and act upon the vision and values of sport.

In the equity and access discussion paper (Sutcliffe and Kirby, 1994:29), equity in sport is defined as the allocation of resources, provision of opportunities and making of decisions "without prejudice or favouritism to any one group." Within this context, equity is equity between the sexes and for minority groups. The provision of equitable sport leads to equitable access for all to the whole spectrum of sport opportunities, opportunities appropriate to individuals in terms of their choice, interest and ability.

The authors go further to define discrimination,[9] systemic discrimination,[10] positive measures[11] and specific to our purposes here:

> [h]arassment is defined as a comment, conduct or gesture directed toward an individual or group of individuals which is insulting, intimidating, humiliating, malicious, degrading or offensive. Harassment is a form of discrimination and is prohibited by the Canadian Charter of Rights and Freedoms. (Heritage Canada 1994:29)

Notice that no direct mention is made of sexual harassment or abuse or any other specific kinds of harassment. There is also no mention of "unwanted" attention based on sex, sexuality or other prohibited grounds for discrimination, a cornerstone of sexual harassment definitions world-wide (International Labour Office 1992). In essence, this definition is instructive only in the most general way. And yet, equity and equitable access are key to establishing a safe, respectful environment for all. In practical terms, a sporting environment that is both equitable and equitably accessible is one with little room for discrimination on the basis of sex, race, disability and so on. It is an environment where participants understand that the highest standards of behaviour are expected and respected.

ATHLETE-CENTRED SPORT

Integral to the response to public pressure to develop a healthy and safe sporting environment has been the education of coaches and athletes about their roles, rights and responsibilities. To date, however, one of the most radical and arguably significant shifts for organized sport in Canada occurred in 1992, when it was proclaimed that sport should be athlete-centred. The introduction of athlete-centred sport has advanced the need to alter fundamentally the framework informing sport and the treatment of athletes. In essence, such a model suggests that sport should be a coach-led but athlete-centred (Canadian Heritage 1994:17). It gives primacy to the need of the athletes and suggests that the sport system as a whole has a number of responsibilities (Clarke 1995:26). And since the concept of athlete-centred care was first introduced, there has been an increased awareness of athletes' rights and the growing expectation among amateur athletes that sport organizations should be "athlete-centred" (Melnitzer 1999:23).

Athlete-centred sport can be interpreted in many ways, including that "excellence means excellence in every aspect of the sport experience," "every athlete deserves a qualified coach," "the health of an athlete is paramount" and "athletes are encouraged to develop and exercise their full range of abilities."[12] The 1992 national sport plan by the Federal/Provincial/Territorial Sport Policy Steering Committee describes athlete-centred sport as follows:

> ... one in which the values, programs, politics, resource allocation and priorities of organizations and agencies emphasize consideration of athletes' needs in a holistic sense, with performance goals set within that context. (Clarke 1995:26)

According to such a model, athletes participate at all levels: developing codes of conduct, formulating policies regarding discipline, harassment and health and safety, and working out training regimes, competition schedules and performance measures. Athletes also determine how much emphasis they want to place on competition. Most importantly, they are more in control of what happens to them in a sport environment, and they fully expect their sport experiences to be positive, to reach their potential, to play fair, to be drug-free and to contribute to the sport system when their athletic careers conclude.

As well, under this model, a new role for coaches is intended to emerge. Coaches are encouraged to use their expertise to facilitate athletes' needs and goals. Specifically:

> They foster and support the development of an athlete. They provide leadership and expertise as athletes strive to achieve their goals of self-development and winning. In the coach-led, athlete-centred system, coaching decisions are based on the long-term holistic development needs of athletes. (Clarke 1995: 26)

Coaches are now held responsible for the well-being of those athletes with whom they are entrusted. This includes understanding how to undertake the role of a coach in a sensitive and ethical manner. In sum, the kind of relationship that should emerge involve a two-way rather than a one-way form of communication (British Institute of Sports Coaches 1989).

In the vision of athlete-centred sport, the potential for the abuse of power is greatly reduced, and coaches are responsible for the empowerment of athletes through provision of positive sport experiences in a healthy environment. The authors of the athlete-centred sport discussion paper were certainly aware of the sexual harassment and abuse issues, and several of them have spoken publicly and forcefully about the need to eradicate such harassment. They made specific reference to harassment in the paper, writing that:

> Harassment is [or ought to be] prevented by educational programs and monitoring. Policies and procedures are in place to deal with harassment, should it occur. Support systems are in place [or ought to be] to assist athletes who have been harassed. (Canadian Heritage 1994:section 3.1.10)[13]

They included provision for a number of mechanisms, including an independent dispute-resolution mechanism, an athlete ombudsperson, and programs for the education, regulation and licensing of coaching, many of which have since appeared in sexual harassment policy recommendations of the National Sport Organisations.[14] Under such a model, the sport system and coaches also have a duty and responsibility to establish an environment free of sexual harassment and abuse.

Indeed, one has to be careful not to place all the responsibility on coaches to realize athlete-centred care. It then becomes too convenient in cases of sexual harassment or abuse to place the blame on atypical, aberrant, or "perverse" individuals (Tomlinson and Yorganci 1997) rather than seeing the problem as systemic. The real importance of the introduction of an athlete-centred model should be seen in the assumption that the entire sport system has responsibilities to its athletes—obligations which go beyond those of an employer—specifically, the good physical and moral development of youth and young adults. Accordingly, an athlete-centred model requires that the entire sport system, including its coaches, see the well-being of athletes as central concerns. It calls for sport organizations' programs and services to be regularly reviewed and evaluated against athlete-centred standards.

Changing an institution as resilient and resistant as organized sport and reorienting those in sport to this new focus takes considerable time and effort. Within the sport context, coaches, athletes and virtually all other participants make judgements based on values—both the values they learn from their sport participation and the personal values which they bring to sport. Tomlinson and Strachan (1997) suggest that one's sense of commitment to the values of sport and one's sense of what is right and wrong (morality) are part of what could be called one's personal ethics. Leadership is more than an individual phenomenon; it's embedded in people's lives and cultures (Greenfield and Robbins 1993, as cited in Tomlinson and Strachan 1996:70). In other words, it is not just poor personal decisions made by individual harassers and abusers which explain the existence of sexual abuse but also that the environment in which people engage in sporting activity influences what behaviours and attitudes are developed and encouraged. Thus, we reject the notion that sexual harassers or abusers are just "individuals gone bad" and accept that organized sport has a responsibility to ensure that a culture of harassment and abuse do not thrive in the sport environment. This is challenging because the context of sport, in particular the powerful "win at all costs" ethos, informs the culture of sport.

Our concern here is twofold. First, if the sport culture is a healthy one, where values are clear and ethics are the foundation of sport practice, toleration of harassment and abuse of any sort would be low. However, if the values are not clear and discussions at the level of principle about the issues facing sport are contra-indicated, toleration for closed-mindedness and discrimination would be increased. Second, when a sport participant is concerned about making good decisions about what is right and wrong and strives to behave in moral ways, it is imperative that the sport environment be supportive. A participant who has a poor personal ethic should find sport a difficult place to function unless that personal ethic is revised. Put another way, in preventing harassment and abuse, it is important that we consider both how the sport environment influences individual participants and how the participants influence the sporting context.

Mike McNamee states that the character of a moral person can be seen as related to the community in which one lives or interacts and that "sport is both developer of moral and immoral character" (1997b:2). The sporting community is, therefore, a critical environment for the development of moral character. Thus, while we may know what is correct and honourable for us personally, if we are fully engaged in sport, our personal ethic may also conform to the values of our sport, and sport becomes a critical site of influence on our personal ethic. So, it could be said that an individual both influences and is influenced by the ethics of the profession (Tomlinson and Strachan 1996:67). By understanding what organized sport intends (sport ethos), through its attempts to describe and live by its values, we can begin to see what happens when conflicts arise, such as when sport does not follow its stated values or when individuals use sport to express sexual motives or seek sexual gratification.

We also find the analogy of the poisoned stream that the Canadian Centre for Ethics in Sport (CCES) uses to be quite instructive on the ethic of care. The CCES suggests that sexual harassment and abuse are pollutants in the flowing stream that is sport. Also clouding the stream are mistrust, disloyalty, the compromise of one's personal ethics, drug abuse and so on.

To bring sport back to life, the very environment in which athletes compete must be freed from pollutants. For organizations committed to reducing the potential for violence, such cleansing involves establishing a safe sport environment and careful training, screening and monitoring of sport personnel. It is through such expressions of the ethic of care that sport can achieve its optimal state: one that is free from drug-abuse, cheating, poor sportspersonship, and discrimination and violence, including sexual harassment and abuse.

Achieving athlete-centred sport is a tall order by any standards; yet sport has committed itself to taking a strong leadership role in this area. In order to achieve a truly athlete-centred approach, fundamental change needs to occur in the world of sport. Values need to be linked to some larger ethical orientation, an ethical framework. Values and ethics go hand in hand. And yet, in the context of sport, little work has emerged on exploring the relationship between the two.

Ethics is the science of morals and is synonymous with words such as integrity, morality, principles and standards. However, as David Gough reminds us, "ethics is not merely a manual of do and don't rules.

Ethics is also an established way of doing things, a shared sense of values, goals and significance" (quoted in Berlow 1994:4). Unlike social ethics, sport ethics is a nascent area of research and application. There is the need for further consideration of ethical frameworks within which sport and, in particular, coaches should operate.

CANADIAN CENTRE FOR ETHICS IN SPORT

One organization specifically charged with clarifying the values described for sport is the Canadian Centre for Ethics in Sport. Centred in Ottawa, this organization exists to ensure that "sport takes place by fair and ethical means." The CCES has spent several years addressing the issues of fair play in sport, drug-free sport, pursuit of sporting excellence and the provision of leadership to a sport system where "ethical conduct is highly valued and practised" (Lachance 1997). In particular:

> The Canadian Centre for Ethics in Sport is charged with the duty of care to our young athletes. We are ready, and committed, to work with the sport community to achieve the goals we all share—sport that is good, sport that is challenging, sport that is ethical, and above all, sport that is a positive and rewarding experience. (CCES 1997:1)

Victor Lachance, Director of the CCES, says that sport, and thus, all those in sport, have a responsibility to ensure that an ethic of care is properly discharged (Lachance 1997). By this, he means that an ethic of care:

> ensures the protection of the well-being of the health and safety of young people whose welfare, by virtue of their participation in sport, must be entrusted to others. Consequently, when such duty is not fulfiled, or when such trust is breached, we must be concerned with the best interests of those who are harmed by this failure of care. (CCES 1997:3)

The CCES interprets the ethic of care to mean that those in the business of sport have obligations beyond those of an employer for the care of sport participants. An ethic of care can therefore be seen to transcend the legal standard of care. According to the CCES, therefore, organized sport has an active duty to provide sport opportunities which develop the physicality and morality of youth and adults.

Lachance does not, on the other hand, consider that a formal inquiry into harassment and abuse in Canadian sport is required. According to Lachance:

you don't need an inquisition, so much as you need an obligation within sport to carry out a duty of care. What's missing is
that collective sense of the sport community's obligation to care
for those who are affected by decisions and services and programs. (*Globe and Mail* January 22, 1997, C12)

It is the clear thinking of the CCES, concentrating on the ethic of
care, fair play, drug-free sport and other ethical issues in sport, which
shows a clarity of role and purpose, and which also has the potential to
challenge sexual harassment and abuse in sport.

Important work in the area has also been undertaken by the University of Toronto. In April 1997, the University of Toronto's Task force
on Intercollegiate Athletics published general principles for guiding athletics at the university. Among these principles is a commitment to en-
hance whole-person development and, in particular, a recognition that
athletic skill and strategic/technical knowledge should be honed as part
of an overall curriculum which strengthens, among others things, an
ethic of caring and service, and an athlete-centred model.

The CCES and the wider sport community recognize an ethic of care
as an important value and emphasize that it ought to be at the very
centre of sport and specifically athlete-centred sport. The core moral
issue is that sport and coaches have a responsibility to care for athletes.
Arguably, however, there is not yet a comprehensive understanding of
the care ethic and how values stemming from this ethic have the potential to transform Canadian sport, including coach-athlete relations.

AN ETHIC OF CARE
The study of an ethic of care has developed from Carol Gilligan's
groundbreaking work *In a Different Voice: Psychological Theory and Wom-
en's Development* (1982). In this work, Gilligan challenges Lawrence
Kohlberg's influential theory of moral development. His framework is
dominated by an ethic of justice and measures moral maturity by an
individual's ability to adhere to rules and universal principles of rights
and justice. This involves seeing onself and others in "universal" and
"general" terms, and one's method of decision-making aims to be impartial, expresses the ideal of equal concern and respect for others and
gives primacy to universal individual rights.

In her research, Gilligan claims to have revealed a different, con-
ventionally unrecognized voice of moral reasoning that she maintains
Kohlberg's psychological measures of moral development fail to properly acknowledge. Gilligan labels this "different voice" as a voice of
care, responsibility and concern for others. She argues that those who
exemplify the "different voice" see themselves defined in a context of

particular relationships with others. Ethical issues are seen as problems within relationships. Gilligan contrasts the different voice, expressing the morality of care, with a voice expressing a morality of justice based on rights, rules and principles by elaborating on what it means to reason in a different voice. She writes:

> In this conception, the moral problem arises from conflicting responsibilities rather than from competing rights and requires for its resolution a mode of thinking that is contextual and narrative rather than formal and abstract. This conception of morality as concerned with the activity of care centers moral development around the understanding of responsibility and relationships, just as the conception of morality as fairness ties moral development to the understanding of rights and rules. (19)

Gilligan further explains that those who reason in a "different voice" distrust "a morality of rights" because of "its potential justification of indifference and unconcern" (2). She argues that unlike ethic-of-justice and rights thinkers, who employ abstract and impersonal decision-making styles, care-based problem solvers often "question the hypothetical" to gather more relevant information in order to better understand the full scope of problems and the practical, material consequences of any decision (Bender 1990:37). In other words, Gilligan maintains that such thinkers are concerned with nurturing others and consequently, are interested in "the social consequences of action" (1982:167).

Many theorists have built upon Gilligan's findings to develop their own conceptions of an ethic of care. Some have associated care with women and their conventional roles and experiences in the private sphere. Many others have taken a broader approach and have attempted to apply such moral and ethical values to social and political institutions of the public sphere. As Sevenhuijsen argues: "political philosophers are beginning to recognize the values of an ethics of care and it has become a subject which can no longer be overlooked by established writers in the fields of ethics and normative political theory" (1998:70). Indeed, the significance of care has been recognized in its application in the fields of nursing (Kuhse 1997), the legal system (Bender 1990; Henderson 1997; Hankivsky 1997), politics and public policy (Tronto 1993; Clement 1996), and environmental reform (Plant 1989). Arguably, an ethic of care also has a largely uninvestigated potential in the world of sport.

What makes an ethic of care unique is that it begins with an assumption of human connectedness. It prioritizes the maintenance of relationships and responsibilities (whether these are relationships between equals or those who are not equal). Instead of being formal and abstract, an ethic of care emphasizes the need for a contextual approach to moral decision-making. Care also entails taking into account concrete situations and the real consequences of any decision. Acting in accordance to care entails striving to improve the situation of others. An ethic of care should thus be understood as both an attitude and actions.[15] Moreover, it is informed by practice and in turn, informs practice. Care can perhaps be thought of as a practical ethic, one which seeks to bridge theory and practice. One of the most comprehensive and effective definitions of an ethic of care has been formulated by Joan Tronto and Bernice Fisher. As Tronto explains:

> On the most general level, we suggest that caring be viewed as a species activity that includes everything that we do to maintain, continue and repair our "world" so that we can live in it as well as possible. (1993:103)

While conceptualizations of care have differed, generally speaking, there are a number of unique elements which can be interpreted as constituting the core of an ethic of care.[16] Arguably, they are also the most relevant for creating athlete-centred care and for transforming the current values and priorities of sport.

Contextual Sensitivity

The first distinguishing element is the priority care gives to contextual sensitivity. Attention to context means taking into account and thoroughly analysing the particular political, economic and social details of people's lives; it requires focusing on the whole person in any decision-making process. Through such a lens, individuals are seen as distinct, but fundamentally social beings who are defined by their relationships, the communities in which they live and by their personal circumstances. The dense contexts of people's lives can only be understood if we consider how people experience the home, workplace, school, church, neighbourhood, mall, recreation centre and gym, and what kinds of social relations are built into these contexts (Rogers 1998:329). Similarly, contextual sensitivity assumes that certain categories of social life—including gender, race, class, ethnicity and geography—structure human realities. Also, personal status—including age, sexual orientation and ability—can impact directly on how persons are differently located in society. These concrete and descriptive details are integral to understanding the unique relational and situational contexts of others' lives. According to a care ethic, such details are essential to the consideration of any problem and for the appropriate resolution of any conflict. As Tronto explains: "no aspects of people's lives or histories need to be left out of [such] discussion"(1993:168).

An approach that is contextually sensitive in sport involves an appreciation of the reality that all key stakeholders are uniquely situated and defined by their relationships and connections to others within the sport community. Specifically, it could have important implications for understanding the dimensions and dynamics of coach-athlete relationships. For example, in the case of female athletes, contextual sensitivity could facilitate a critical understanding of sex and gender (prescriptive, socially constructed roles and expectations linked to power and privilege), and their related determinants. These construct the social position and reality of the female athlete and help us to better comprehend the inherent power imbalances between a female athlete and her male coach. So, contextual sensitivity would encourage an understanding of the female athlete as differently located, with less power and status in society and within the sporting world by virtue of her gender and position as athlete.

Responsiveness and Trust

Grasping contextual details in given situations, however, also requires an element of responsiveness to others in their uniqueness (needs and competencies) and their own particular terms. According to Noddings (1984, 1993) it is more difficult to know another's nature, needs and desires when one holds power over the other. Partially this is because caring responsiveness involves refraining from any paternalistic behaviour and instead, respecting others as equals with whom we share human relations. In the words of Beane "when we care about others, we do not simply act for people (on their behalf) as 'objects' of our care, but also with them as mutual 'subjects' in the human experience" (1990:62).

Responsiveness calls for careful listening to the needs and desires of others as they define and articulate them. It can involve acknowledging the legitimacy and worth of the stories of those who experience vulnerability and inequality. As Tronto explains:

> Responsiveness suggests a different way to understand the needs of others rather than to put our selves into their position. Instead, it suggests that we consider the other's position as that other expresses it. (1993:134)

Similarly, Colleen Sheppard alludes to the dynamics of responsiveness when she argues that "caring ... involves responding to the needs of others based on efforts to be attentive to and empathize with their needs and desires as they define and articulate them" (1992–93:324).

Responsiveness also requires individuals to recognize when they have special obligations and responsibilities to others. Some may understand responsiveness and respect as synonymous in such a context. For example, Dillon argues that "respecting persons involves valuing and responding to others in their concrete particularity" (1992:115). Moreover, Dillon sees respect as proactive and positive. She also argues for example that "respect requires not so much refraining from interference as recognizing our power to make and unmake each other as persons and exercising this power wisely and carefully" (116). The moral precept of responsiveness requires that we remain alert to the possibilities for abuse that arise with relationships of vulnerability. As Tronto effectively explains, "we must constantly evaluate whether we are being overly protective, too unresponsive, too reliant on our assumed expertise and so on" (1993:14). This necessitates not just seeing a person in terms of their rights but actually responding to them in ways that exceed our responsibilities to them. This way of interacting, attentive listening and being empathetic to those who may be vulnerable to harms, injustices and abuses may also result in a decision to remove oneself from a particular relationship or situation involving care. As Sevenhuijsen explains, responsiveness may also necessitate deciding not to provide care because one possesses insufficient means to meet or satisfy self-expressed needs or because they conflict too strongly with one's own needs or moral convictions (1998:83).

Responsiveness places athletes front and centre, because it depends on listening and being attentive to athletes' experiences, needs and feelings—as athletes themselves define and articulate them. Tronto puts it succinctly when she observes that "care forces us to think concretely about people's real needs [as those who experience discrimination explain them] and about evaluating those needs" (1993:124). In practice, responsiveness can protect and promote the dignity of athletes. Athletes may feel that they are empowered to affect change in sport. And because coaches and others in positions of power are required to recognize and respond to the self-identified needs and concerns of athletes, responsiveness may also lead to more trust and respect within the coach-athlete relationship.

Consequences of Choice

Lastly, the ethic of care necessitates a consideration of how our choices impact on others. Gilligan argued that the application of a morality of justice in decision-making is susceptible to "indifference" and "unconcern" for others. It is generally agreed that, when using the framework of an ethic of care, decisions are not made by relying upon abstract and impartial rules and principles. This is because an ethic of care is concerned with all possible outcomes and with the practical and material effects on people's lives of making certain decisions. Both Clement and Tronto emphasize that explicit in an ethic of care is a responsibility to make connections of how those around us (both in the private and public spheres) may be affected by our actions.[17] In other words, an ethic of care prioritizes evaluating the impact and consequences on real people of making certain choices and decisions.

Perhaps the most important aspect of this third principle is the attention it places on promoting the well-being and preventing the harm and suffering of others. Indifference and lack of concern are replaced by caring responsibility. It is about more than good intentions. It is about actively assessing all possible harmful consequences of certain decisions. For example, it raises awareness of how self-esteem, self-confidence and self-respect can be nurtured or alternatively destroyed in relationships of trust such as those between coaches and athletes. It may also encourage coaches to understand how inappropriate action towards an athlete can have ripple effects through the entire sporting community, impacting negatively on other athletes in the care of the coach, on the reputation of the particular sport, and in the end, on all members of the sporting community and beyond. The individual coach's roles and responsibilities are therefore conceptualized within the context of society and the entire sporting community. In the words of Webb-Dempsey (1996:95): "caring moves self-determination into social responsibility, and employs knowledge and strategic thinking to decide how to act in the best interest of others. Caring binds individuals to society, to their communities and to each other."

CONCLUSION

The core elements of care—an emphasis on contextuality, the priority of responsiveness to others and otherness, and concern with the actual outcomes of decision-making—have largely been absent from the sport culture. Most relevant to achieving athlete-centred sport and informing coach-athlete relations is that care appears to provide guidance on how to deal with the concrete situations of human relations and the complicated moral dilemmas that people often experience in intimate relations. These include issues surrounding dependency, responsibility, vulnerability and trust—"the fragility of intimacy and connectedness and that ever-recurring problem of establishing boundaries between the self and others" (Sevenhuijsen 1998:3).

We must be aware that an ethic of care is only effective in the context of liberal, pluralistic, democratic institutions (Tronto 1993:158). We are not proposing that an ethic of care is a replacement for the law or for policies, protocols or codes of ethics addressing sexual harassment and abuse. They are a necessary minimum requirement. We are proposing, however, that care can provide a wider ethical framework within which to better understand these provisions, their significance and their application. In other words, such policies, protocols and codes of ethics would benefit from being embedded in the vocabulary of care. As Tronto explains,

> to include the value of caring in addition to commitments to other liberal values (such as a commitment to people's rights…) makes citizens more thoughtful, more attentive to the needs of others, and therefore better democratic citizens. (1993:169)

Arguably, rules and regulations which are framed within the context of an ethic of care can be truly transformative, creating a safe environment for athletes.[18] This is because the above mentioned elements of care can contribute to more effective identification of and a critical understanding of harassment and abuse. Through its values and priorities, a care ethic clearly condemns violence, whether in the form of sexual abuse or harassment. Care can therefore provide the sporting community with an ethical framework for developing common values, responsibilities, behaviours and attitudes—the kind of group identity and sense of shared values which are largely absent from sport culture. An ethic of care can provide the foundation for strengthening the collective will of the sporting world in responding to harassment and abuse. It can also build a sense of community in which every member is expected to devote themselves to the internal goals and values that together they share and for which they are jointly and separately responsible (Arnold 1997 :15).

NOTES

1.   Although the focus of this chapter is on coach-athlete relationships and in particular the abuse of power by coaches, sexual abuse and harassment occurs among athletes, can be instigated by athletes on coaches and can involve other key players in sport, including sport psychologists, officials, chaperones, parent-helpers, volunteers, administrators, caretakers, transportation workers, etc.
2.   See section 153 of the *Criminal Code*.
3.   Important work in the domain of abuse prevention has also been undertaken by the Canadian Red Cross under its Abuse Prevention Services, initially developed in 1976. It targets adolescents as well as professionals and community members.
4.   Established in 1997, the collective represents forty national sport organizations and governments, including the Canadian Hockey Association

(CHA), the Coaching Association of Canada (CAC), the Canadian Centre for Ethics in Sport (CCES), and the Canadian Association for Women and Sport and Physical Activity (CAAWS).

5. Some, such as the Canadian Professional Coaches Association, have developed specific codes of ethics for coaches.
6. This list is derived from McNamee 1998.
7. The inquiry was established in response to the drug use by the sprinter Ben Johnson at the 1988 Olympics which led to the stripping of his Olympic medal.
8. In October 1993, the CBC revealed examples of harassment and abuse in volleyball, swimming and rowing. The program prompted a response from the national sport community and a harassment in sport working group was formed with representatives from CAAWS, Sport Canada, Volleyball Canada, CIAU, Althetes Canada, the Canadian Sport Council, CPCA, CAC, and Status of Women Canada.
9. "Discrimination refers to differential treatment that results in disadvantage for those who have received the differential treatment. A disadvantage could be exclusion from participation" (Sutcliffe and Kirby 1994:29).
10. Systemic discrimination occurs when established policies and practices of a system (or organization) result in disadvantage to marginalized groups (Sutcliffe and Kirby: 29).
11. Positive measures are special measure undertaken to redress any imbalance stemming from past discrimination, and to respond to identified needs of those who have been disadvantaged. (Sutcliffe and Kirby 1994: 29).
12. Some of these are from the personal coaching experience of one of the authors; others are from the athlete-centred sport discussion paper (Canadian Heritage 1994: 18-19).
13. At the suggestion of Mike McNamee, we have added "ought to be" twice in this quote to illustrate the difference between reality and intent. A different definition of harassment is provided later in the equity and access discussion paper. We will be drawing a comparison between them subsequently.
14. Amongst the signature characteristics for an equitable and accessible athlete-centred system are monitoring, recruitment, promotion and retention of members from designated equity groups; representation of designated groups in decision-making, delivery of positive measures; and anti-harassment work (where all sport organization members are familiar with procedures for dealing with harassment complaints). At those points where sport organizations are held accountable for their progress on the achievement of these, harassment comes up at least as a procedural measure.
15. This same position is taken by Joan Tronto and Selma Sevenhuijsen.
16. These are drawn from the conceptualiztion of care found in the works of both Joan Tronto (1993) and Grace Clement (1996). Clement, for example, argues that the key features of an ethic of care are its contextual decision-making, its priority of maintaining relationships and its social concept of self as connected in relation to others. Tronto's elements of care resonate with some of those of Clement and include: attentiveness to the needs of others, responsibility to care, competence in care-giving and responsive-

ness to the other's position as the other expresses it (Tronto 1993:see pages 127–137).

17. Clement for instance argues that: "many people beyond our family and friends are also particularly vulnerable to our actions and choices and thus the ethic of care has implications beyond our sphere of personal relations" (1996b: 73).

18. Both these goals are necessary and seemed to be heightened by the latest Supreme Court decisions in The Children's Foundation et al. v. Patrick Allan Bazley and Randal Jacobi and Jody Saur v. Boys' and Girls' Club of Vernon and Harry Charles Griffiths.The judgement in the first case rendered any clubs, schools and treatment centres liable for sexual attacks on children in their care even if they did not behave negligently. This availability of vicarious liability as a legal tactic (i.e., by demonstrating that the environment in which the abuse occurred contains sufficient elements of risk) has potential implications for the Canadian sport community.

Chapter Five

Retracting the Dome of Silence

Sexual abuse and harassment of athletes are significant problems that have been under-acknowledged to date. We have proposed some explanations for this, focusing on the values and imperatives that underpin sport and illustrating the power of these features in securing and perpetuating the silence surrounding these issues. We have argued that these features have led to sport being one of the last major social institutions to be scrutinized and exposed with respect to sexual abuse issues.

Over the past few years, several incidents of sexual abuse and harassment, child molestation and sexual assault in the sporting context have come to light. As in all interpersonal and relationship violence, it can be safely assumed that these reported cases are only the tip of the iceberg and that most cases remain hidden. Some of the individuals who have been victims have participated in criminal or civil suits against their perpetrators. Some have settled for public exposure in the media. The public and sport communities have reacted with typical, initial responses of shock, denial, anger and disbelief. As can be seen in the comments of the athletes surveyed in this study, the personal emotional costs can be life-long and serious. Even so, early responses from sport organizations often focused mainly on risk management and reducing liability by instituting screening, training and protocol development for staff and volunteers. Some sport organizations or associations have focused on particular elements within their sport, such as coaching or

Coach. He is, as Mary Magdalene sings in *Jesus Christ Superstar*, 'just a man.' No longer my coach, my god." (p. 193)

inter-athlete behaviour. Recently, some sport organizations have responded with more comprehensive foundational codes of ethics and behaviour. It is clear that the issues of sexual abuse, harassment and assault are important to athletes, sport organizations, their governing bodies and the public.

There is no doubt that increasing awareness has led to increasing activity in sport intended to reduce sexual abuse and harassment of athletes. However, there is a necessity both to do more to protect athletes, their families and the public and to define a shared set of ethical principles that will build a more caring sport institution. In Chapter Four we described the principles of an ethic of care and how they could be applied to sport. We discussed the importance of athlete-centred care and equitable sport and the efforts of several organizations to achieve these goals. In this chapter we argue that sport would benefit from an even deeper understanding of an ethic of care and its application to sport. In addition, we argue that the underlying imperatives directing sport also need radical changes, in order to thoroughly integrate and support a sport-specific ethic of care.

Systematic changes in the philosophical and conceptual underpinnings of sport are required to set the stage for safe and truly liberatory athletic experiences. Retracting the dome of silence will involve many steps. Of high importance is the element of opening up the issues for scrutiny, shedding light on the formerly private sphere of intra-team and interpersonal relations, and claiming this terrain as public. This process is long overdue in sport. However, the trend has clearly begun.These changes will ensure that the elements of an ethic of care— context, responsiveness, and consequences—become embedded in sporting organizational response and would serve as a foundation for developing codes of behaviour, responses to incidents and public goal-setting. However, it is also essential to transform the imperatives and underlying values that currently direct sport into more positive forces, so that the enhanced ethic of care will be shared and supported across the institution of sport. This requires that the fundamentals of sport that are currently shared and assumed be interrogated and revised. Without this move, the efforts to create an ethic of care for sport and the resulting codes of conduct will ultimately drift unanchored.

What are these radical shifts that could transform the sport institution and thereby reduce sexual abuse, harassment and other negative experiences for athletes? The responsibility for identifying problems and solutions must become shared collectively across the entire institution of sport and across society. This would de-emphasize individual responsibility for illuminating abuses and inequities, and, in particular, remove it from the athletes' shoulders. This needs to be accomplished while reaffirming the individual responsibility of the coach or trainer as part of their duty as an employee or responsible volunteer.

This would also de-emphasize or eliminate the established trend toward creating internal mechanisms for resolution of problems, and instead place the resolution process firmly in the public domain. Having sport-based policies and protocols and dealing with complaints in-house is indicative of the strength of the powerful imperatives propelling sport. However, it also illustrates the need for sport organizations to limit the exposure and control the treatment of negative incidents. Melnitzer (1999) describes the extent to which sport organizations have gone to respond to sport complaints and further athletes rights in Canada.

This trend has been somewhat good for athletes in that it heightens procedural fairness and due process, and consequently increases the safety of amateur sport for athletes. In parallel, this has heightened awareness in sport organizations to manage risk and reduce liability. However, this approach is currently contained within the sport organization system. As Melnitzer describes it, this "self-contained internal administrative process adhering to principles of natural justice" is well developed in Canadian amateur sport, which will presumably increase the protection of athletes' rights (1999:24). Establishing internal mechanisms for resolution has not been specific to sport. Universities, for example, have long held internal hearings and investigations into sexual harassment complaints in an extra-judicial framework. Such approaches slow the development of full institutional accountability and transparency, and often serve to protect the goals and images of the institutions. In such processes, the development of an ethic of care that will reduce inequities, acknowledge consequences and heighten awareness of the context of problems and their solutions will be delayed or inhibited.

A second major shift in the sport culture that would alter the context of sexual abuse and harassment is the eradication of all forms of violence. Violence has a pervasive presence in and around sport. It is essential to see that a continuum of cultural acceptability of violence invades the conceptual bases of some sports, the practice of some sports, and the behaviour of some spectators. Accomplishing this shift would mean eliminating in-sport violence, such as fighting and harmful checking in ice hockey, most boxing and wrestling, bullfighting, and other sport activities where the actual expectation of the activity includes harm or fighting. Additionally, this would mean the introduction of zero-tolerance for abusive and violent fan behaviour, such as verbal abuse of players, fan hooliganism and rioting. Finally, this reversal of the expectation and acceptance of violent behaviour would extend to abusive behaviours within sport, sexual or otherwise, that serve to intimidate, silence or emotionally hurt athletes.

When one considers the entire spectrum of violent behaviour—verbal and emotional abuse, heckling, hazing, initiation rites, physical intimidation and retaliation, sexual abuse and assault—one sees that nonviolent, peaceful sport is increasingly rare. Further, these activities are currently supported by a culture of violence, where players and fans alike live amidst swearing, vandalism, violent television programming and film, and war. This particular shift will be very difficult to achieve, but if it could be, sport would serve as a true model of non-violent activity and would acquire the moral goodness and superiority historically attached to it.

Changing this element requires the rethinking of the values and practice paradigm of modern sport. Are there elements of sport practice as basic as competition, trophies, titles and financial incentives that work against an open and humane sport culture, free of abuse and violence? Are there any revolutions in store to reclaim the joy of sport, the thrill of performance and the comradeship of team work without the punishing "thrill" of hazing and humiliation or the vicarious "pleasure" for fans of observing violent behaviour on the ice or playing field? Some argue that the entire notion of violence in sport is merely reflective of and contributary to the mixture of power and gender relations that make up patriarchal systems. As Bennett et al (1987:378) state: "Sport serves as a training ground for maintaining the domination/submission relationships characteristic of patriarchy."

In this framework, eliminating the elements of violence in sport will be a difficult task. Lenskyj (1992b:22–24) offers ample argument for drawing this conclusion. She argues that the expectation of and tolerance for sexually aggressive behaviours and sexual assaults by male athletes "suggests that it is seen by some as a natural extension of the physically aggressive behaviour of male athletes during the game" (24). Eventually, such sexually violent behaviour among male athletes transmutes into male coach behaviour and attitudes as the athletes become coaches. Gagnon assesses the link between the essence of sport culture and the prevalence of domestic violence against women in society. She maintains that both violence in sports and violence against women have traditionally been "immune" from significant criminal charges (1997:65). After interviewing a small sample of both violent and non-violent men about their thoughts and experiences in sport, she identifies competition, hierarchy and performance valorization as key elements of sport culture that had affected them. Both groups of men perceived links between male socialization and violence, particularly violence in sports.

Indeed, among the violent men who were in therapy for such behaviour, there was a tendency to retreat from involvement in sport to facilitate positive changes.

All of these themes raise challenging questions for sport and for the social and governmental home to sport institutions. Will there be pressure and prosecutions, not only about individual cases of sexual abuse, but also on team hazing and humiliations (as initiation rites), after injuries in the "normal" practice of sport (i.e., concussions in hockey), and on parent, fan and spectator hostilities (i.e., profanity and fist fighting)? Will there be a swell of opinion that will create these changed attitudes and demand some analysis and changed behaviours among sport organizations, athletes and fans alike? Most certainly there will not be unless there is leadership within the institution of sport that will responsibly and openly interrogate the current paradigm and its foundational assumptions of violence.

A third shift, concerning the financial elements of sport, is more pragmatic. Funding, insurance and sponsorships of sport should be explicitly tied to evaluations that measure ethical standards of care and conduct. Some of this information could be derived from asking athletes about their experiences. Any money channelled to sport organizations should be conditional upon clear outcomes and formative evaluations of the activities of the organization. This would set and maintain standards of relations that ideally could protect individuals from assuming over-responsibility for negative experiences and shift such responsibility to the collective shoulders. Items such as policies, rules, codes of care and conduct and experiences of athletes could be assessed annually in order to establish the viability of the organization as a positive force.

Another part of this shift concerns legal and moral rectification. If there continues to be more and more legal and compensatory liability attributed to sport organizations and institutions as a result of cases being brought forward, then it is certain that there will be a forced overhaul of the vision and practice of sport. The criminal and civil justice systems will demonstrate the extent to which sport organizations, their sponsors and employees may be held passively or actively responsible for the violations that occur under their management. While the therapeutic aspects of this are one thing, the economic impact on the institutions themselves will be the real site of change. If and when massive compensatory payouts are being made to resolve individual and class actions following abuse and violence, leaders and shapers of policy and practice in sport will be forced to take notice.

The same pecuniary pressures will be brought to bear on procedural reform in sport. For example, institutions or organizations wishing to protect themselves from liability will want to demonstrate their protective policies, their support for safe disclosure procedures and their staff and volunteer training programs. Screening of volunteers and employees will need to be shown to be effective, and real consequences brought on perpetrators and organizations that protect them. Such consequences could include delisting from support, league affiliations or sponsorships. Sponsors of sport may want assurance of protective policies to prevent damage to their images. Governments will be under pressure to justify public expenditure on sport if there are not complete assurances that it is safe and ethical. Finally, government and non-government sport agencies alike will press for specific evaluations and standards that will guarantee safety to athletes. All of these trends are inevitable if there is continued disclosure of abuse by individuals and groups of athletes. The true test of the sport institution in Canada will be in its speed and willingness to champion individuals who bring abuse complaints, instead of resisting them, and to encourage actions instead of defence.

Another element worth addressing is the issue of sex segregation in sport and how its entrenchment (or in some cases, re-entrenchment) could contribute to increased safety. The current model, with mainly male coaches of female athletes and all-female teams, presents an increased danger of sexual exploitation. If there were more sport carried out with same-sex coaches, there might be a decrease in the amount of male-perpetrator–female-victim sexual abuse. This is not as predictable a way to protect young males, however, as much of the abuse that they report was perpetrated by older men. Nevertheless, the match between the sex of the coach, trainers and related personnel and athletes is an important issue to revisit for several reasons that extend beyond protecting (particularly female) athletes.

A shift in the assumptions about mixing sexes would also increase opportunities for women coaches. At the moment, women fill a minority of coaching positions, illustrating occupational inequity for females and limited role modelling for young female athletes. These elements alone highlight the serious inequities in sport for women and girls. If women were required or preferred for coaching and training positions with female athletes or female teams, then opportunities would open up and safety would be increased.

Further, cultural assumptions about sex and sexuality often exist uncritiqued in the structure of sport. For example, figure skating dance pairs are assumed to be male/female duos. Obviously heterosexual in design, the sport promotes in its very structure and practice a cross-gender interaction and quality. The costumes, the steps, the moves and the judging perpetuate and reward the heterosexual assumption underlying the sport. In the Gay Games of 1994, held in New York City, the appearance of same-sex ice skating dance pairs was novel. In addition to demonstrating obvious opportunities for gay and lesbian athletes, this paradigm calls up for question the automatic assumption of mixed-sex pairings in sports such as ice dancing. In addition, watching same-sex ice dance partners perform inexorably leads to questioning old assumptions about costumes, steps, judging and fan responses. Many other gender and sex-related assumption could be re-evaluated, not only to increase safety in sport, but also to offer increased opportunities for career development of coaches and trainers, role modelling for athletes and freedom for cultural expression and difference in the way sport is practised.

There is need for a critical reassessment of the examples of extreme heterosexuality and hypersexuality that are evident in sport. Certain male dominated sports such as weightlifting, hockey or boxing stress macho imagery, aggression and over-developed muscles. There is often an assumption that successful male athletes are also extremely sexually active and have excess sexual energy. Such female dominated sports as beach volleyball, synchronized swimming and gymnastics rely on sexist uniforms and mannerisms and imposed body images. These elements often coexist with assumptions that female athletes are passive, even while sexual, and are there in part to sexually entertain while they perform their sport.

These examples demonstrate the currency of an exaggerated sexuality that still informs some aspects of competitive sport. In the interests of developing a more athlete-centred and ethical sport, it may be time to change this imperative and to replace it with a more neutralized sexuality that would be more affirming and inclusive of all participants. In addition, it would send a very different message to audiences, trainers, coaches and sport administrators.

A final paradigm shift is more practical. Reviewing and redefining "consent" is long overdue, not only in sport, but in all arenas where sexual harassment is a possibility or fact. Currently, consent is often loosely interpreted. Imperfect and incomplete definitions abound with respect to what consitutes "consent" to sexual relationships. For example, if there is no force involved and/or if the parties both desire the sexual encounter or relationship, some have argued that sexual harassment and abuse principles do not apply. This view completely ignores the power and gender relations that define human social interactions. It ignores potential abuses of authority that exist when relationships based on an activity or affiliation (such as sport or work or education) are converted into sexual relationships. It also ignores the functional aspects of relationships (such as evaluator, trainer, protector, teacher, coach) that are thrust into a distorted context or put into jeopardy as soon as a sexual relationship begins. Finally, some relationships described as "consensual" even ignore the issue of age differences and the legal definitions surrounding criminal behaviours regarding sexual relationships with minors and children.

Uncertainty about defining the limits of sexual harassment is still widespread. There are many examples of ambiguous codes regarding sexual harassment. McNamee discusses this point with reference to various sport codes (1998:154–56). In his analysis of the code developed by the National Coaching Foundation in the United Kingdom, he notes that the wording states:

"Coaches should not condone or engage in sexual harassment ... with performers or colleagues. It is considered that sexual relationships with performers are generally inappropriate to the professional conduct of coaches." The word "generally" immediately introduces ambiguity into the moral equation. As McNamee concludes, this word reduces the impact of the rule from a principle that is absolute to a guideline that is porous. Even among feminists and anti-violence advocates steeped in defining and responding to sexual violence, there is ambiguity about such boundaries. Somehow, the idea of "consent" gets redefined when both parties report that they wanted the relationship, that they entered into it willingly and that it superseded their working or functional relationship. Sometimes consent is dependent on timing—for example, parties are considered free to consent unimpeded after two years of ceasing the professional relationship. This is the approach in several professional codes, such as that of the American Psychological Association.

We would argue that consent should be much more clearly defined and that codes of behaviour across society's institutions need to be revamped accordingly. Codes of consent cannot, in our view, be amorphous or time-limited in their application and interpretation. Elements of authoritative and power relations remain even after the formal functional relationship between two people ends. Dependency for past or current benefits may colour the so-called "consensual" nature of the relationship, even post-team membership. Recognition of the long-term impacts of imbalanced relationships that result when gender, power and authority are mixed is central to redefining consent. If sport takes up this challenge across its organization and laces a stricter definition of consent into an ethic of care for sport, it will be a leader in moving sexual harassment codes of conduct into a new sphere.

Such new codes should include explicit limits of sexual relationships between those with large age differences, between minors and adults, and in any relationship where trust, dependency and authority are still elements of the relationship. These codes should be defined and enforced outside of the sport organization, to avoid collusion and to prevent professional protection from entering into the processes. In sport, there is the added challenge of defining behaviour to cover both professional and voluntary personnel, because much of sport is based on contributions of voluntary labour. A notable example of consent re-definition is embedded in the United States Olympic Committee's Coaching Code of Ethics. In this code, explicit directives regarding sexual intimacies with current and former athletes, as well as with current and former sexual partners, are clearly laid out. Further, even though sexual relations are allowed after a two-year post-coaching interval, there are six factors that must be satisfactorally considered and explained to al-lay any fears of undermining public confidence in the coaching profes-sion and the institution of sport. These six factors include:

1.   the amount of time that has passed since the coach-athlete relation-ship terminated;
2.   the circumstances of termination;
3.   the athlete's personal history;
4.   the athlete's current mental status;
5.   the likelihood of adverse impact on the athlete and others; and
6.   any statements or actions made by the coach during the course of the coach-athlete relationship suggesting or inviting the possibilty of a post-termination sexual or romantic relationship with the ath-lete or coach.

CODES FOR THE FUTURE

The broad base for future codes must include recognition of an ethic of care and its underlying principles. In addition, this ethic of care must evolve with and reflect an ethical transformation within the institution of sport. In this section we review the essence of a sporting ethic of care, note some positive examples of caring codes already in existence and suggest some directions for further development.

The idea that an ethic of care provides important methodological precepts for rethinking sport has also been also put forward by Arnold, who states that "acting rightly in sport ... is as much a matter of caring and motivation as it is of reasoning"(1997:71). He asserts that caring in sport:

> ... involves more than a concern for the preservation of sport as a valued human practice in some abstract sense, but a concern about the manner in which sport should be conducted at an inter-personal level. It entails a whole range of emotions, feel-

ings and sentiments that are concerned with the interests and needs of all participants, both on and off the field of play. Caring involves an ability to perceive another in a particular way— as a person with whom one is in relation whether as a comrade or competitor, in a shared enterprise mutually agreed upon. Caring involves the emotions—a capacity to feel for or empathize with the state of another. At the heart of caring is a concern for the welfare of one's fellow participants and a disposition to act towards them in a benevolent way. (72)

With its values—especially the prioritizing of respect, responsiveness and responsibility—an ethic of care provides a solid foundation on which the renewal of sport can begin. In practical terms, an ethic of care can provide a framework against which sport policy and programs can be evaluated and can provide a basis for the kind of transformative change which needs to occur within the context of sport to reduce harassment and abuse.

At a minimum, in responding to issues of sexual harassment, an ethic of care can:

1. encourage the sport community to commit to make sport better;
2. frame the debate about sexual harassment and abuse in ethical terms;
3. foster the well-being, health and safety of athletes, families and community members; and
4. support and assist those who have been harassed and abused.

There are a number of multi-sport organizations that have demonstrated leadership in developing ethically driven codes, policies and principles (e.g., AthletesCAN, Canada Games Council, Canadian Association for the Advancement of Women in Sport, Coaches Association of Canada, Canada Professional Coaches Association, Canadian Commonwealth Games Society, Canadian Interuniversity Athletic Union, Canadian Athletes Association and Canadian Hockey League). Effective leadership is imperative for such policy approaches to be developed and supported by the sport community. Moreover, a number of sport organizations in Canada and the United States have captured some of the moral precepts of care, especially in emphasizing responsiveness/ trust to others and otherness, in their guiding principles.

The Canadian Professional Coaches Association
The Canadian Professional Coaches Association, an arm of the Coaching Association of Canada, has produced *Coaching Code of Ethics: Principles and Ethical Standards,* that "concern the broader aspects of the

sport experience, incorporating morals, values and ethics"(Werthner 1995:8).

The code sets out number of guiding principles for the conduct of coaches:
1. Respect for participants—challenges coaches to act in a manner respectful of the dignity of all participants in sport.
2. Responsible coaching—ethical expectation that the activities of coaches will benefit society in general and participants in particular and will do no harm. Fundamental to this principle is the notion of competence (maximizing benefits and minimizing risks to participants).
3. Integrity in relationships—coaches are expected to be honest, sincere, and honourable in relationships with others.
4. Honouring sport—challenges coaches to recognize, act on, and promote the value of sport for individuals and teams and for society in general.
With regards to sexual relations:
2.17 Be acutely aware of power in coaching relationships and therefore, avoid sexual intimacy with athletes, both during coaching and during that period following coaching when an imbalance in power could jeopardize effective decision-making.

Canadian Olympic Association

A Code of Ethics for the Olympic Family: "The Olympic Commitment" Principles:
1. Act fairly: Consider the interests of others as well as your own, treat people justly, equitably and appropriately.
2. Do no harm: We have an obligation to avoid actions that harm others.
3. Act with respect for self and others: Respect for oneself means acting with integrity, and choosing and living up to your values. Respect for others includes considering their interests, choices and opinions.
4. Keep your agreements: Many of our interactions with others contain unspoken agreements or contracts. ... This is the basis of the moral values of honesty and integrity.
5. Reason consistently: A moral reason for you to act is a moral reason for anyone to act in the same way in similar circumstances.

Coaching Association of British Columbia
Coaching Code of Conduct:
The athlete/coach relationship is a privileged one. Coaches play a critical role in the personal as well as athletic development of their athletes. They must understand and respect the inherent power imbalance that exists in this relationship and must be extremely careful not to abuse it. Coaches must also recognize that they are conduits through which the values and goals of a sport organization are channelled. Thus, how an athlete regards his/her sport is often dependent on the behaviour of the coach.
3a) Refrain from the use of profane, insulting, harassing or otherwise offensive language in the conduct of his/her duties.
7) Regularly seek ways of increasing professional development and self-awareness.

Coaches must:
1. Ensure the safety of the athletes with whom they work.
2. At no time become intimately and/or sexually involved with their athletes. This includes requests for sexual favours or threat of reprisal for the rejection of such requests.
3. Respect the athlete's dignity; verbal or physical behaviours that constitute harassment or abuse are unacceptable.

Canadian Hockey League
In 1997, the Canadian Hockey League published a report, *Players First*, which makes recommendations regarding screening processes, educational strategies, policy implementation, policy and complaint processes, counselling and support services, on-ice conduct and confidentiality. A commitment to protecting its players from harassment, abuse and discrimination informs this policy document (8).

Canadian Curling Association
In its 1995 *Policy on Harassment*, the Canadian Curling Association includes a section entitled "Accountability Framework." It says:

Harassment is a form of discrimination. It is prohibited by the Canadian Charter of Rights and Freedoms and by Human Rights legislation in every province and territory of Canada. In most extreme forms, harassment can be an offence under Canada's Criminal Code. The sport of curling accepts its obligation to be proactive in addressing this sensitive issue by:
• establishing policy to reflect organizational values,
• resolve any situation expeditiously and fairly,

- recognize that harassment in any form is a safety issue,
- recognize that excellence in sporting achievement is not possible within an environment marked by harassment,
- educate through policy and program initiatives,
- acknowledge that the coach-athlete relationship is a most privileged one, dependent on trust and respect. No person should have to choose between participation in sport with abuse or quitting sport to remove abuse.

The United States Olympic Committee

Some sport organizations in the United States have also demonstrated an approach which is ethically driven. The United States Olympic Committee's *Coaching Code of Ethics*, mentioned previously, articulates the following general principles underpinning its coaching code:

This Code is intended to provide both the general principles and the decision rules to cover most situations encountered by coaches. It has as its primary goal the welfare and protection of the individuals and groups with whom coaches work. This Code also provides a common set of values upon which coaches build their professional work.

Principles:
A) Competence: Coaches strive to maintain high standards of excellence in their work. They recognize the boundaries of their particular competencies and the limitations of their expertise.
B) Integrity: Coaches avoid improper and potentially harmful dual relationships
C) Professional Responsibility: Coaches uphold professional standards of conduct, clarify their professional roles and obligations, accept appropriate responsibility for their behaviour, and adapt their methods to the needs of different athletes.
D) Respect for Participants and Dignity: Coaches respect the fundamental rights, dignity, and worth of all participants.
E) Concern for Others' Welfare: Coaches seek to contribute to the welfare of those with whom they interact professionally.
F) Responsible Coaching: Coaches are aware of their professional responsibilities to the community and the society in which they work and live. Coaches try to avoid misuse of their work. Coaches comply with the law and encourage

the development of law and policies that serve the interest of sport.

In addition to the explicit factors regarding sexual activity post-termination of the coach-athlete relationship that were discussed above, an extremely comprehensive and clear sexual harassment guideline for coach-athlete relations appears in The United States Olympic Committee's *Coaching Codes of Ethics*,[1] under the section "Ethical Standards: Training Athletes." Excerpts are:

> 3.04 Sexual Intimacies with Current Athletes
> Coaches do not engage in sexual intimacies with current athletes.
> 3.05 Coaching Former Sexual Partners
> Coaches do not coach athletes with whom they have engaged in sexual intimacies.
> 3.06 Sexual Intimacies with Former Athletes
> a) Coaches should not engage in sexual intimacies with a former athlete for at least two years after cessation or termination of professional services.

Caring Policies and Codes

An ethic of care promotes the importance of heathy, respectful relations free from burden, hurt or suffering. To facilitate these ends, policies should be short, accessible and straightforward. While there are examples of guidelines for developing harassment policies (i.e., the Law Society of Upper Canada and the Canadian Association for the Advancement of Women in Sport), we suggest that policies that fully reflect the priorities of an ethic of care would also include the following components:

- explicitly stated responsibility of the sport organization for the implementation of their harassment/sexual harassment policy. This should include proactive prevention and intervention measures that the organization is committed to in their institutional response to sexual harassment and abuse, including support for both victims and their families;
- description of all possible relations in which harassment/abuse may occur, including detailed description of inappropriate coach-athlete relationships (such as those found in the United States Olympic Committee's *Coaching Codes of Ethics*);
- a practical step-by-step guide to what victims can do to deal effectively with the harassment or abuse they may be experiencing.

These three principles alone would help to locate the responsibility for abuse and harassment, contextualize a definition of abuse and harassment, and articulate and offer responsive mechanisms for complaints. These elements combined offer a minimal basis for integrating ethic-of-care principles into abuse and harassment policies in sport. Although increased development of rules and regulations pertaining to sexual harassment and abuse in sport is essential, there is typically a delay between articulation of such rules/policies and real cultural change. We recommend that to maximize operational effectiveness, policies must be developed with input from all stakeholders and contextualized within a broad code of ethics that reflects the sporting community's adherence to a shared sense of values and goals. The ability to appeal to commonly shared principles is critically important in a public endeavour such as sport, where it is essential to ensure that basic moral rights are protected and public expectations of good are met. The ethic of care with its focus on responsiveness to others, contextuality, and concern with the actual impact of decisions has the potential to change the paradigm of sport and in particular, the paradigm of power relations in coaching.

Following the moral precepts of care, codes of ethics would yield the following guiding principles for the conduct of coaches in an athlete-centred model of sport:

- Recognize your potential to do harm: The well-being and health of athletes are paramount as are the active prevention and relief of their burden and suffering.
- Act responsively: Consider the potential impact/consequences of your choices and decisions on your sport and sport in general.
- Be responsive to the needs of others: Be attentive to the needs of the athlete as the athlete himself/herself expresses them.
- Honour your obligations: Recognize your special obligation and responsibility to an athlete, and respect codes of conduct, rules and laws regarding behaviour.
- Understand power: Use your power wisely and remain alert to the possibilities for abuse within a coaching relationship

While an ethic of care can provide common values to help frame the debates around sexual harassment and abuse policies, it will not eliminate sexual harassment and sexual abuse from sport. However, establishing a conscious ethic of care to underpin policy and protocol development will establish an elevated basis for sport responses to abuse and harassment issues. By articulating and prioritizing values traditionally not emphasized by the sport world, an ethic of care can create a more complex understanding of sexual harassment and abuse and thereby allow the athlete-centred model of sport to reach its full potential. A contextualized and subtly sensitive definition of abuse and harassment and responsive mechanisms for complaints will allow the athlete to more safely operate in the sporting environment.

WHAT ELSE NEEDS TO BE DONE?

In addition to the fundamental changes discussed above, there are other actions required to improve the sporting climate with respect to the issues of sexual abuse and harassment. First and foremost, there is an immediate need for more research to determine the prevalence of sexual abuse and harassment on a sport-by-sport basis, both in Canada and internationally. In addition to quantitative study, it is essential to carry out qualitative research, in order to assess the texture of the experiences for athletes in different sporting contexts. This approach would allow the particular qualities and characteristics of different sports to be identified and assessed with respect to sexual abuse and harassment. Training contexts and pressures and other elements such as coaching behaviours and amount of body contact may have an impact. Rates of abuse may differ in individual and team-oriented sports. Once such information is gathered, more specific remedies can be developed and undertaken by the respective sport organizations and governing bodies. Further, such work will undoubtedly fuel more revelation and disclosure from current and former athletes.

In addition to establishing baseline rates of sexual abuse and harassment, it is also necessary to investigate and evaluate the development of policy and protocol that has been carried out in various sports and sport organizations, not only in the high performance context, but in all levels of sport in Canada. In the final analysis, the insights gathered from such investigations will undoubtedly lead us to a more critical look at professional sport as well. With respect to the suggested shifts in paradigms articulated above, there is much that professional sport could examine in the interests of promoting a more positive and moral sporting example. There is much to be learned about the relationship of the various sporting levels on this continuum from community leagues to pro sport, but it seems likely that the links exist on both positive and negative aspects of sporting life.

A final area requiring intensive investigation relates to access to justice for athletes. Help-seeking patterns of athletes, as well as their experiences with various paths of retributive justice, need to be documented. Further, the issues of therapeutic jurisprudence, in particular the experiences of athletes with the various mechanisms of redress, need to be analyzed. Such information is crucial for both the athletes and their families, as well as those giving help and advice to athletes who may have experienced sexual abuse or harassment. The pros and cons of taking justice-seeking measures can cross a wide range. There are different motivations or needs for justice depending on the circumstances or the individual, and these different needs may best be met through different modes of justice or retribution (see Feldthusen, Hankivsky and Greaves 2000). It is important to clarify what the experiences of athletes are with internal investigative mechanisms, criminal courts, civil courts, and human-rights and ombudsperson investigations. Were the needs and expectations of the athlete met or were they thwarted? Comparison with other types of claimants would also assist sport in coming to develop the best restorative justice mechanisms for its athletes.

Once these issues are researched in both Canada and other countries, it will be possible to develop adequate international policy responses which will have a wider impact on the international sporting community. To accomplish this, comparative research between different nations using the same operational definitions would be most enlightening. In general, the goal of developing effective and safe protocols and policies as well as rewarding and therapeutic judicial responses is crucial, and could best be shared between nations.

Other actions that could be initiated without the need for further research include such things as much more systematic screening and training of volunteers. While heavy reliance on volunteers presents some difficulties, e.g., less control via labour codes and the employer-employee relationship, the issue of quality must be addressed. Parents and athletes in particular will require assurances in order to move forward with their support for the sporting organizations with which they are involved. Certainly, assurances of effective screening and training for all personnel will be required by insurers concerned with liability for sport organizations. Evaluations will need to be undertaken of the education programs, protocols and policies that are in place to determine whether they are effective. The issues regarding internally based mediation and retributive mechanisms must also be addressed. These are several actions in both the research and protocol and policy arenas that could be addressed immediately to diminish the costs of sexual abuse and harassment in sport from all parties' points of view.

CONCLUSION
Sport is an institution that has assumed a moral goodness. As Berlow (1994:4) states, "Society ... draws inspiration from watching the progress of sports, believing that sports are played according to a higher and more worthy set of rules." However, it is clear that sport embodies nega-

tive behaviours, such as abuse, drug taking, homophobia and sex discrimination, and imperatives and values that have questionable impact, such as competition and patriotism. And it is precisely because of the assumptions of moral and physical superiority attached to sport that these negatives are often held in high relief. Arnold argues that sport is characterized as much by the moral manner in which it is conducted, as it is by the pursuit of its particular skills and activities. He says that: "sport, despite its more recent perverted and unsavoury connections, is a culturally valued practice that embodies some of the highest human ideals and most cherished traditions" (1997:15). We would argue that it is precisely these presumptions about sport that have protected it from scrutiny so far and left many of its negative elements without full illumination. The "unsavoury connections" to which Arnold refers include violence, abuse, drug taking, doping, cheating and aggression. While this book has concentrated on analysing the issues of sexual abuse and harassment, the overriding need for an improved ethic of care would benefit all of sport and assist in responding to and eliminating all of these practices.

As Tomlinson and Yorganci point out, the overriding gender and power relations "have been forces for the preservation of the status quo in sport, and of some of the hidden and injurious consequences of that status quo" (1997:136). They go on to challenge sport organizing bodies to review their own cultures in this light, and be less likely to dismiss negative incidents as mere aberrations (137).

A key element of the sport culture that has a direct and strong effect on sexual abuse and harassment is the notion of community. In its pure manifestation, it reflects the team-building and shared commitment to excellence and success that is entrenched in sport. As Arnold describes it: "when a person enters into sport as a practice he or she becomes a member of an extended community ... which is distinguished by its fraternal bonds and commitments" (1997:15). Arnold goes on to say that such goals create not only a sense of shared identity and a framework for nurturing, but also a sustained morality. In its shadow side, it is the familism and clan-like pressures that keep secrets and create shame. As we have seen, victims of sexual abuse and harassment are particularly vulnerable to the pressures of family: loyalty, emotional commitment and isolation. It is this feature, particularly in the context of male perpetrator/female athlete victimization that creates silence, confusion and long-term damage. Consistent with our findings, Tomlinson and Yorganci report that sexual harassment and abuse are often not recognized as such by its victims, even when they are presented with definitions of abuse and harassment which match their own experiences (1997:146).

If the voices of the athletes in this book are to count, real changes must soon be made in the organizations that govern sport. The social and psychological climate that is created for the victims of sexual abuse and harassment in sport will be the key factor affecting the speed of the retraction of the dome of silence. If it is positive, more and more voices will be heard. More and more examples will come to light, some old, some new. More cases will be tried and civil suits begun. More class actions will be organized and more sport organizations will be forced to respond. Most important, more individuals will reveal their pain and humiliation for the purpose of improving the overall moral climate in sport.

NOTE
1.   The approach, structure and content of this *Coaching Code of Ethics* were inspired by the Ethical Principles of Psychologists and Code of Conduct, December 1992 (American Psychological Association, vol. 47, n. 12, 1597–1611, the British Institute of Sport Coaches (1989) and the NCAA.

References

"Accusations díagressions physiques et sexuelles contre des religieuses díun orphelinat pour filles de Terre-Neuve." *La Presse* (February 26, 1997): E-7.

American Psychological Association. *Ethical Principles of Psychologists and Code of Conduct: Reports of the Association* 47, 12 (December 1992): 1597–1611.

Arnold, Peter. *Sport, Ethics and Education.* London, UK: Cassell, 1997.

"At three reform schools: Sexual abuse survivors suing provincial government." *Daily News* Amherst, Nova Scotia, (April 2, 1997):14.

Beane, J.A. *Affect in the Curriculum: Toward Democracy, Dignity, and Diversity.* New York: Teachers College Press, 1990.

Bella, Leslie. *The Christmas Imperative: Leisure, Family and Women's Work.* Halifax, NS: Fernwood Publishing, 1992.

Bender, Leslie. "From gender difference to feminist solidarity: Using Carol Gilligan and an ethic of care in law." *Vermont Law Review* 15, 1 (Summer 1990): 37.

Bennett, Roberta, K. Gail Whittaker, Nina Jo Woolley Smith and Anne Sablove. "Changing the rules of the game: Reflections toward a feminist analysis of sport." *Women Studies International Forum* 10, 4 (1987): 369–379.

Berlow, Lawrence. *Sports Ethics: A Reference Handbook.* Santa Barbara: Contemporary World Issues, ABC-CLIO, 1994.

Board, Mike. "You'll do anything to accomplish that dream." *Ottawa Citizen* (January 7, 1997): C6.

Brackenridge, C.H. "Ethical concerns in women's sport." *Coaching Focus* 6, (Summer 1987): 57.

———. "Crossgender relationships: Myth, drama or crisis." *Coaching Focus* 16, (Spring 1990): 46.

———. "Sexual harassment and abuse in sport: 'It couldn't happen here.'" Cheltenham and Gloucester College of Higher Education, Cheltenham, UK, Unpublished paper, 1993.

———. "Fair play or fair game? Child sexual abuse in sport organizations." *International Review for the Sociology of Sport* 29, (1994): 287–299.

———. "Healthy sport for healthy girls? The role of parents in preventing sexual abuse in sport." Paper presented at the PreOlympic Scientific Congress, Dallas, TX, July11–15, 1996a.

———. "The Pedophile and the predator." Paper presented at the International PreOlympic Scientific Congress, Dallas, TX, July 11–15, 1996b.

———. "Dangerous relations: Men, women and sexual abuse in sport." Inaugural Lecture, Cheltenham & Gloucester College of Higher Education, Cheltenham, UK, March 17, 1997a.

———. "'He owned me basically...': Women's experiences of sexual abuse in sport." *International Review for the Sociology of Sport* 32, 2 (1997b): 115–130.

———. "Sexual harassment and abuse in sport." In G. Clarke and B. Humberstone (eds.), *Researching Women and Sport.* London: Macmillan Press, 1997c, 126–141.

———— *Spoilsports: Understanding and Preventing Sexual Exploitation in Sport*. New York: Routledge, forthcoming, 2001.

Brackenridge, C.H., and S.L. Kirby. "Playing safe: Assessing the risk of sexual abuse to elite child athletes." *International Review for the Sociology of Sport— Special Issue on Youth Sport*. 1997.

————. "Protecting athletes from sexual abuse in sport: How theory can improve practice." In R. Lidor and M. Bar-Eli (eds.), *Sport Psychology: Linking Theory and Practice*. Israel: Wingate Institute, 1999: 261–279.

Brackenridge, C.H., D. Summers and D. Woodward. "Educating for child protection in sport." In L. Lawrence, E. Murdoch and S. Parker (eds.), *Professional and Development Issues in Leisure, Sport and Education*. Brighton: Leisure Studies Association, No. 56, 1995, 167–190.

British Institute of Sports Coaches (BISC). *Code of Ethics*. London, 1989.

Buchanon, Carrie. "U. of O. investigates student-teacher relationships: Philosophy professor's ethics are called into question." *Ottawa Citizen* (March 21, 1997): B1.

CBC. "Crossing the line: Sexual harassment in sport." *The Fifth Estate*. November 2, 1993.

————. "Hazing." *The Fifth Estate*. November 1996.

Canadian Association for the Advancement of Women in Sport and Physical Activity (CAAWS). *Gender Equity Handbook*. 1992.

Canadian Council for Drugfree Sport. *Doping Control Standard Operating Procedures*. n.d.

Canadian Council for Ethics and Sport (CCES). Educational material. 1995 .

————. *Discharging an Ethic of Care*. January 29, 1997.

Canadian Curling Association. *Policy on Harassment*. Gloucester, ON, 1995.

Canadian Freestyle Ski Association. "What to do in a sexual harassment emergency." Gloucester, ON, 1993.

Canadian Heritage. *A Planning Framework for Sport in Canada: A Joint Document of the Sport Community and Federal/Provincial/Territorial Sport Committee* (FPTSPSC), Ottawa, October 1994.

Canadian Hockey League. *Players First Report*, Canada, n.d. Retrieved March 26, 1999, from http://www.slam.ca/PlayersFirst/home.html

Canadian Panel on Violence Against Women. *Changing The Landscape: Ending Violence: Achieving Equality: Executive Summary and Final Report*. Ottawa, 1993.

Casswell, D.G. *Lesbians, Gay Men and Canadian Law*. Toronto: Edmond Montgomery Publications Limited, 1996.

Christie, J. "Sport leaders reject inquiry into sex abuse." *Globe and Mail* (January 22, 1997): C12.

Clarke, Heather. "Athlete-centred sport—An athlete's point of view." *Coaches Report* 2, 2 (Fall 1995): 26.

Clement, Grace. *Care, Autonomy and Justice*. Boulder, CO: Westview Press, 1996.

"Coaching, trust and sex." *Coaches Report*, 3, 3 (Winter 1997): 5.

College of Physicians and Surgeons of Ontario. *The Preliminary Report of the Special Task Force on Sexual Abuse of Patients of the College of Physicians and Surgeons of Ontario*. Toronto, 1991a.

————. *The Final Report of the Special Task Force on Sexual Abuse of Patients of the*

College of Physicians and Surgeons of Ontario. Toronto, 1991b.

Corbet, Rachel. *Harassment in Sport: A Guide to Policies, Procedures and Resources.* Gloucester, ON: Canadian Association for the Advancement of Women in Sport and Physical Activity, September 1994.

Dillon, Robin S. "Respect and care: Toward moral integration." *Canadian Journal of Philosophy,* 22, 1 (March 1992): 105–131.

Donnelly, P. (with E. Caspersen, L. Sergeant and B. Steehhof). "Problems associated with youth involvement in high performance sport." In B.R. Cahill and A.J. Pearl (eds.), *Intensive Participation in Children's Sports,* American Orthopaedic Society for Sports Medicine, Champaign, Illinois: Human Kinetics Publishers (1993): 95–126.

Dubé, Francine. "Women accuse teacher of abuse." *Ottawa Citizen* (April 22, 1997): A1.

Elliott, M., K. Browne, and J. Kilcoyne. "Child sexual abuse prevention: What offenders tell us." *Child Abuse and Neglect* 19, 5 (1995): 579–594.

Fairholm, J. (ed.). *Speak Out! ... Act Now! A Guide to Preventing and Responding to Abuse and Harassment in Sport.* Gloucester, ON: Canadian Hockey Association, 1997. Retrieved June 25, 1999, from http://harassmentinsport.com.

Fasting, K. "Sexual Harassment in Sport." Invited keynote Speech to the conference: Physical Education and Sport in a Global Context: Honoring the Legacy, Charting the Future. 50th Anniversary Conference IAPESGW, Smith College, Northampton, MA, July 7–10, 1999.

Feldthusen, B., O. Hankivsky and L. Greaves. "Therapeutic consequences of civil actions for damages and compensation claims by victims of sexual abuse." *Canadian Journal of Women and the Law* 12,1 (2000).

Findlay, H., and R. Corbett. "What is harassment?" In J. Fairholm, J. (ed.), *Speak Out! ... Act Now! A Guide to Preventing and Responding to Abuse and Harassment in Sport,* Gloucester, Ontario: Canadian Hockey Association, 1997. Retrieved June 25, 1999 from http://harassmentinsport.com/Handbook/Sec1ch2.html.

Finkelhor, D. *Sexually Victimized Children.* New York: Free Press, 1979.

"Former boy scout sues over sex assault." *Toronto Star* (March 9, 1997): A-11.

Frank, Blye. Personal communication. Mount Saint Vincent University, Halifax, Nova Scotia, June, 1993.

Friedman, Marilyn. "Beyond caring." In M.J. Larrabee (ed.), *An Ethic of Care: Feminist and Interdisciplinary Perspectives.* New York: Routledge, 1993.

Fusco, C. "Lesbians and locker rooms: Challenging homophobia." *Canadian Women Studies/les cahiers de la femme* 15, 4 (1995): 67–70.

Fusco, C., and S.L. Kirby. "Are your kids safe?: Media representations of sexual abuse in sport." In S. Seratton and B. Watson (eds.) Sport, Leisure and Gendered Spaces. LSA Publication No. 67 (2000).

Gagnon, N. "Sport culture and violence against women: Between pleasure and barbarism." *Institut Simone de Beauvoir Institute, Review/Revue* 17 (1997): 61–72.

Gilligan, Carol. *In a Different Voice: Psychological Theory and Women's Development.* Cambridge, UK: Cambridge University Press, 1982.

Gonsiorek, J.C. (ed.). *Breach of Trust: Sexual Exploitation by Health Care Profes-*

sionals and Clergy. London: Sage, 1995.

Greaves, L. *Smoke Screen: Women's Smoking and Social Control*. Halifax: Fernwood, 1996.

Greenfield, T., and P. Ribbins (eds.). *Greenfield on Educational Administration: Towards a Humane Science*. London: Routledge, 1993.

Hankivsky, Olena. *The interpretation of equality under the Charter of Rights and Freedoms*. Ph.D. dissertation, University of Western Ontario, Department of Political Science, London, ON, 1997.

Haysom, Ian. "B.C. man faces child-sex charges: Raid on home nets video on bestiality." *Ottawa Citizen* (March 7, 1997): A5.

Henderson, Lynne. "Legality and empathy." *Michigan Law Review* 85 (1987): 1574–1653.

Herman, J. *Trauma and Recovery*. New York: Basic Books, 1992.

Hodgkinson, Christopher. *Educational Leadership: The Moral Art*. Albany: State University of New York Press, 1991.

Holman, M. *Female and male athletes' accounts and meaning of sexual harassment in Canadian interuniversity athletics*. Ph.D. dissertation, Michigan State University, July 14, 1995.

International Professional Development Program Tour (IPDP). *The Way ahead for Canadian Women in Sport*. The Report of the 1992 IPDP Tour. Gloucester, ON: Tait Mckenzie Institute, Canadian Sport and Fitness Administration Centre, 1993.

International Labour Office. "Combating sexual harassment at work." *Conditions of Work Digest* 11, 1 (1992).

Jimenez, M. "Coach gets two and one-half years for sexual assaults." *Edmonton Journal* (December 1, 1993): A1.

———. "Running coach says he never had sex with young athletes." *Edmonton Journal* (November 25, 1993): B1.

Joyce, S. *The Chilly Climate for Women in Colleges and Universities*. London, ON: University of Western Ontario's Caucus on Women's Issues and the President's Standing Committee for Employment Equity, 1991.

Judo Canada. *National Team Handbook*. 1997.

Kelly, L., R. Wingfield, S. Burton and L. Regan. *Splintered Lives: Sexual Exploitation of Children in the Context of Children's Rights and Child Protection*. Essex: Bernardo's, 1995.

Kirby, S.L. *High performance female athlete retirement*. Ph.D. Dissertation. University of Alberta, Edmonton, AB, 1986.

———. "Not in my back yard: Sexual harassment in sport." Paper presented at the Commonwealth Games Congress, Victoria, BC, 1994. Published in *Canadian Women Studies/Les cahiers de la femme* 15, 4 (1995): 58–62.

———. "Women, sport and health: 19th century corsets to 20th century olympics." Presentation at the University of Winnipeg, Winnipeg, MB, March 1997.

Kirby, S.L., and L. Greaves. "Foul play: Sexual harassment in sport." Paper presented at the Olympic Scientific Congress, Dallas, TX, July 11–15, 1996.

———. "Le jeu interdit: le harcélement sexuel dans le sport." *Recherches Féministes* 10, 1 (1997): 5–33.

Kirby, S.L., and A. LeRougetel. *Games Analysis*. Ottawa: CAASW Occasional

Papers, 1992.

Kirke, Gordon I. *Players First*. Gloucester, ON: Canadian Hockey League, 1997.

Krause, Renate. Panelist, CAASHHE Conference, Halifax, Nova Scotia, November 20–23, 1996.

Kuhse, Helga. *Caring Nurses: Women and Ethics*. Oxford: Blackwell Publishers, 1997.

Law Society of Upper Canada. *A Recommended Personnel Policy Regarding Employment-Related Sexual Harassment and the 1994 Guidelines of Harassment in Sport: A Guide to Policies, Procedures and Resources*. Canadian Association for the Advancement of Women in Sport and Physical Activity, 1994.

Lachance, V. Executive Director, Canadian Council for Ethics in Sport. Personal communication, Ottawa, January 23, 1997.

Lenskyj, H. *Female Participation in Sport: The Issue of Integration versus Separate-but-Equal*. A Discussion Paper. Ottawa: Fitness and Amateur Sport Womenís Program/Programme pour les femmes de Condition physique et Sport amateur, 1984.

————. *Out of Bounds: Women, Sport and Sexuality*. Toronto: Women's Press, 1986.

————. "Sexual harassment: Female athletes' experiences and coaches' responsibilities." *Sport Science Periodical on Research and Technology in Sport* (Coaching Association of Canada) 12, 6, Special Topics (1992a): B1.

————. "Unsafe at home base: women's experiences of sexual harassment in university sport and physical education." *Women's Sport and Physical Activity Journal* 1, 1(1992b): 19–33.

————. *Women, Sport and Physical Activity: Selected Research Themes*. Ontario: Sport Canada, 1994.

Levine, Naomi. "Sexual harassment and fiduciary trust." CAASHHE Conference, Halifax, Nova Scotia, November 20–23, 1996.

Loland, S., and M. McNamee. "Sport, fairness and play: Plural values and shared ethos." (Draft), In S. Loland and M. McNamee (eds.) *Values, Education and Cultural Diversity, Leicester University*. London: Cassell, 1997.

Mackinnon, C. *The Sexual Harassment of Working Women*. New Haven, CT: Yale University Press, 1979.

Mascoll, P. "Man sexually assaulted 200 boys: Court may jail worst pedophile for rest of life." *Toronto Star* (May 31, 1994): A4.

McNamee, MJ. "Everything you wanted to know but were too afraid to ask: Alasdair MacIntyre." *PSSS* (Philosophical Society for the Study of Sport) *Newsletter* (1996): 8–10.

————. "Rules, trust and professionalism: Some cautionary notes." Draft, unpublished manuscript, 1997a.

————. "Values." (Draft.) In A. Guttman et al. (eds.) *Encyclopaedia of World Sport*. Boston: ABC Clio Press, 1997b.

————. "Celebrating trust: Virtues and rules in the ethical conduct of sports coaches." In M.J. McNamee and J. Parry, (eds.), 1998.

McNamee, M.J., and J. Parry (eds.). *Ethics and Sport*. London: E & FN Spon, 1998.

Melnitzer, Julius. "This sporting life: Lawyers in amateur sports." *Canadian Lawyer* (March 1999): 23–29.

National Film Board. *The Nitinaht Chronicles*. 1997.

Nelson, Mariah Burton. *Are We Winning Yet? How Women are Changing Sports and Sports are Changing Women*. New York: Tandom House, 1991.
———. *The Stronger Women Get, The More Men Love Football*. New York: Harcourt Brace, 1994.
Noddings, Nel. *Caring: A Feminine Approach to Ethics and Moral Education*. Berkeley: University of California Press, 1984.
———. "Ethics from the Standpoint of Women." In Deborah L. Rhode (ed.) *Theoretical Perspectives on Sexual Difference*. New Haven, CT: Yale University Press, 1990. Reprinted in Marilyn Pearsall (ed.), *Women and Values: Readings in Recent Feminist Philosophy*. Second edition. Belmont, CA: Wadsworth, 1993.
O'Hanlon, M. "Victims complaining: courts too easy on sex-abuse doctors." *Daily News*, Amherst, Nova Scotia (April 1, 1997): 4.
Paraschak, V. "Organized sport for Native females on the Six Nations Reserve: Ontario from 1968 to 1980." *Canadian Journal of History of Sport* 21, 2 (1990): 20–80.
Parker, L., Canadian Council for Ethics in Sport. Personal Communication. June 27, 1997.
Pike-Masteralexis, L. "Sexual harassment and athletics: Legal and policy implications for athletic departments." *Journal of Sport and Social Issues* 19, 2 (May 1995): 141–156.
Plant, Judith (ed.). *Healing the Wounds: The Promise of Ecofeminism*. Toronto, ON: Between the Lines, 1989.
Pronger, B. "Football teaches violence." *University of Toronto Bulletin* 5 (January 2, 1993): 20.
Rich, Adrienne. "Compulsory heterosexuality and lesbian existence." *Signs* 5 (1980):631–60.
Richard, Brenda. Panelist, CAASHHE Conference, Halifax, Nova Scotia, November 20-23, 1996.
Rinehart, Dianne. "Rape victim's mother angry sports policy not drawn up." *Vancouver Sun* (November 28, 1996).
Robertson, Sheila. "Coaching, trust and sex." *Coaches Report* 3, 3 (1997): 5.
Robinson, L. Personal communication. Winnipeg, MB, April–July, 1977.
Rogers, Mary F. *Contemporary Feminist Theory*. Boston: McGraw Hill, 1998.
Samuels-Stewart, V. Panelist, CAASHHE Conference, Halifax, Nova Scotia, November 20-23, 1996.
Sevenhuijsen, Selma. *Citizenship and the Ethics of Care: Feminist Considerations on Justice, Morality and Politics*. London: Routledge, 1998.
"Sex, lies and volleyball." *Chicago Tribune* (February 1996): 81.
Sheppard, Colleen. "Caring in human relations and legal approaches to equality." *National Journal of Constitutional Law* 2 (1992-1993): 3–24.
Sport Canada. *A Planning Framework for Sport in Canada*. Ottawa: Sport Canada, 1994.
Statistics Canada. "The Violence against Women Survey: Highlights." *The Daily*, Thursday, November 18, 1993.
Statistique Canada. "Les Femmes au Canada: Portrait Statistique, Rapport," 1995, cat. no. 89-5-3.
Street, L. *The Screening Handbook: Protecting Clients, Staff, and the Community*.

Ottawa: Canadian Association of Volunteer Bureaux and Centres, 1996.
"Stopping sexual abuse in sport: What Canada's coaching leaders are doing." *Coaches Report* 3, 4 (Spring 1997).

Sutcliffe, Judy, and S.L. Kirby. "Equity and access paper," developed on behalf of the Canadian Heritage. *A Planning Framework for Sport in Canada: A Joint Document of the Sport Community and Federal/Provincial/Territorial Sport Committee.* Ottawa (October, 1994).

Thompson, S. *Servicing sport: The incorporation of women's labour for the maintenance and reproduction of a social institution.* Ph.D. Dissertation. Australia, University of Murdoch, 1994.

Thompson, S. *Mother's Taxi: Sport and Women's Labor.* New York: State University of New York (SUNY), 1999.

Tomlinson, P., and D. Strachan. *Power and Ethics in Coaching.* Ottawa: National Coaching Certification Program, 1996.

———. *Handbook: Power and Ethics.* Prepared with the assistance of an Advisory Committee of John Bales (CAC), Tom Kinsmen (CPCA), Marion Lay (CAAWS) and Dan Smith (Sport Canada). Ottawa: National Coaching Certification Program, 1997.

Tomlinson, A., and I. Yorganci. "Male coach/female athlete relations: Gender and power relations in competitive sport." *Journal of Sport and Social Issues* 21, 2 (May 1997): 134–155.

Tronto, J., and B. Fisher. "Toward a feminist theory of caring." In E.K. Abel and M. Nelson (eds.). *Circles of Care: Work and Identity in Women's Lives.* Albany: State University of New York Press (1990).

Tronto, J. *Moral Boundaries: A Political Argument for an Ethic of Care.* New York: Routledge Press, 1993.

United States Olympic Committee. *Coaching Ethics Code.* Colorado Springs, CO, 1996. Retrieved March 26 1999 from http://www.olympic-usa.org/inside/coaching.html

Volkwein, K. "Sexual harassment in sport: Perceptions and experiences of female student athletes." Paper presented at the PreOlympic Scientific Congress, Dallas, TX, July 11–15, 1996.

Webb-Dempsey, J., B. Wilson, D. Corbett and R. Mordecai-Phillips. "Understanding Caring in context: Negotiating borders and bariers." In D. Eaker-Rich and J. Van Galen (eds.), *Caring in an Unjust World: Negotiating Borders and Bariers in Schools.* Albany: State University of New York Press, 1996.

Wells, Mary. *Canada's Law on Child Sexual Abuse : A Handbook.* Ottawa : Communications and Public Affairs, Dept. of Justice Canada, 1990.

Werthner, Penny. "A forum on ethics." *Coaches Report* 2, 2 (Fall 1995): 8.

Wittig, M. "The category of sex." *Feminist Issues* 2, 2, (Fall, 1982): 63–68.

Working Together in Sport and Activities for Children and Coaches. North Kesteven District Council, North Kesteven Sport Development and Lincolnshire County Council, North Kesteven, UK, 1997.